Unique Journeys, 1905

Unique Journeys, 1905

o the Far East with Alice Roosevelt and E.H. Harriman

PATRICIA M. ALMOND

BELLE ISLE BOOKS
www.belleislebooks.com

The publisher does not assume any responsibility or legal liability for the accuracy of the documentation herein.

ISBN: 978-1-947860-62-9
LCCN: 2026900462

Printed in the United States of America

Published by
Belle Isle Books (an imprint of Brandylane Publishers, Inc.)
5 S. 1st Street
Richmond, Virginia 23219

belleislebooks.com | brandylanepublishers.com

EDITOR'S NOTE

I wish I could say that all the books I've had the pleasure of working on were written by great writers, but that's simply not the case. Pat Almond was a rare gift to me in that way. Though we were separated in age by almost sixty full years (which certainly led to some differences of opinion when it came to writing history for modern times), I very much enjoyed discussing the craft of writing with Pat, and she had a real, true talent for it.

In fact, she wrote my favorite sentence of all time. I'm not exaggerating. As soon as I read it, I knew. I found myself repeating it over and over, reading it aloud to anyone who would listen—ask my husband, my mother, my grandfather, all of my associates, and most of my friends.

It's simply this: "In a group picture of proper young ladies, Alice would have been the one out of focus."

It may not seem particularly special after one read, but read it again. Think about what it tells you about Alice, about the time in which she lived, about what was expected of her and what she was instead. It says so much with just one image and very few words. It is the definition of craft, written exactly as it should be. It's not flashy—it has no words over two syllables, no words that have to be looked up in a dictionary. It is simple. And yet, as an experienced book editor and a lifelong reader, I can honestly say it is one of the most clear, succinct, creative, and descriptive sentences I've ever read. And I did not have to edit a single bit of it; it came to me that way.

Pat passed away in early 2022, just as she was finalizing the design of this book. I am still not over the fact that she spent so many years working on a book that she would never see published. I don't think I ever will get over it. She deserved to hold it in her hands.

She invited me to her home for a meeting early on in the editing process, and though I don't make it a habit to go to author's homes, I went. She was ninety-three at the time, and as we talked about her life and her vision for the book, she made us a simple lunch of sliced tomatoes and cheese omelets. I can still taste it: the sun-warm tomato she had picked from her own garden, the melted American cheese tucked inside a pillow of egg lightly seasoned in a cast-iron skillet. Only three ingredients on a plain white plate, nothing imported or expensive or secret. It was divine.

And I think that's what I want to say: that Pat knew how to perfect a thing. It seems that all her life experience had taught her that it wasn't important to make a fancy thing, but to make a good thing; not to make a simple thing extravagant, but to make a simple thing perfect. You don't need big words, you don't need a long list of ingredients. You need time, you need focus, and you need to do a thing with love.

Thank you for that, Pat.

-Mary Peyton Crook

ACKNOWLEDGEMENTS

Without the people whose names are listed below, you would not be reading this book.

First is my grandmother, May Hendrickson McKnight, who organized my grandfather's papers, mementos, and pictures of his trip to the "Far East." She packed them away safely. Next, my mother, Mary McKnight Malmar, preserved them during the sixteen years she had custody. Without those records, this book would not have been written.

Doug Blue, Karen Jones, Paul Stimpson, Ellen Harris, Wendy Harris, and the late Pat Perkinson all provided editorial advice. Mary-Peyton Crook did the painstaking and time-consuming final edits that saved me from many a blunder.

Librarians Betty Dillehay, Racquel Ott, Patricia Baird, and Belinda Buie helped me track down elusive material while Tom Bartron and Tim O'Brien were sources of sanity-saving computer help.

Doug Carr of the Chesapeake Bay Writers could always come up with the name of an appropriate person for any type of help required.

My sister and brother-in-law, Connie and Tom Harris, contributed research at the Library of Congress and years of unending encouragement.

To each: many, many thanks!

Table of Contents

PREFACE

I am not a historian, and this is not, primarily, a history book. It is, rather, an account of the adventures of two groups of travelers who journeyed to the Far East as the Russo-Japanese War was inching to a close early in the twentieth century. Heading one group was a private businessman with a planet-sized vision for expanding U.S. interests. Heading the other was one of the U.S. president's cabinet secretaries, charged with two missions: one public; one secret. The two groups traveled separately and covered some of the same ground, but experienced the Far East from different perspectives.

Among the travelers in one group was my grandfather, John Calvin McKnight, whose letters, journals, and record of the trip became the inspiration for this book.

Like the first installment of a serial, his words drew me in and led me to explore further, to learn about the second group, and to realize that there were wonderful tales to tell, stories that would be meaningless if not set in the context of the war, the peace negotiations, and the widening involvement of the United States in the Far East. The U.S. had grown since the Civil War, from a struggling young nation to a world-class industrial power. Its expansionist president was itching to extend the country's reach and would not be unhappy to see the U.S. recognized as a mover and shaker on the international scene.

"Avoid foreign attachments and entanglements," George Washington had warned in his farewell address. He urged the country to enjoy its isolated position and remain neutral, in order that the fledgling nation might increase its strength as it matured. And by and large, the country followed his advice, eschewing foreign alliances and conflicts until the very end of the nineteenth century, when it allowed itself to be drawn into a war against Spain over Cuba's wish for independence. At that turning point, the U.S. discarded its isolationism as one might toss out an outworn garment. Eventually, a contingent of the U.S. Navy under Commodore Dewey defeated the Spanish fleet in Manila Bay. With the end of the Spanish-American War, Cuba became independent, but the Philippines did not, and the U.S. had become a colonial power. Though some Americans were opposed to the idea of an American empire, others were not displeased with the idea of having access to the island's raw materials and markets. For better or worse, by the turn of the century, the U.S. was ensconced on the Far Eastern scene, with interests to protect.

Meanwhile, on the Asian mainland, the Russian government had obtained from the Chinese the right to build a north-south railroad in Manchuria. With a further concession from the Chinese, the Russian navy was able to berth its battleships at its own naval base at Port Arthur, also in Manchuria. Russian officials were courting the ineffectual Korean emperor. The Japanese government saw Korea as belonging in its own sphere of influence and was increasingly unhappy with Russia's incursions. The Russo-Japanese War was the result.

The conflict, with its trench warfare, use of machine guns, desperate sieges, horrendous casualties, and mammoth naval battle, could be considered a dress rehearsal for World War I, which began nine years later. World War I thrust the Russo-Japanese conflict into the shadows. Most of us are aware that the Russo-Japanese War occurred, but learned few of its details, implications, or the extent of U.S. involvement in the affairs of the Far East.

In early 1905, plans for a group of U.S. senators and congressmen to visit the Philippines began to percolate, but it was July before they departed. In mid-August, a smaller, privately arranged group of Americans sailed for the Far East. By the time both groups returned at the end of October, these travelers had enjoyed an array of experiences in Japan, China, Korea, Manchuria, and the Philippines that could never be duplicated.

The two sets of travelers were drawn from American political and business elites and, in the years that followed, an unusually large number of them (plus several Americans they encountered en route) made serious marks on American public life.

This is the story of their adventures and the events that surrounded them.

PART I

A LIFETIME OF MEMORIES

Yokohama, Japan
October 13, 1905

The October breeze that swept across Yokohama Harbor carried the heavy smell of coal dust overlaid with the tang of salt air, the telltale aromas of a busy port. Dozens of one-man craft, sculled by upright figures in breech clouts, bustled about the harbor, intent on their destinations. A small tugboat full of passengers pulled up alongside the *S.S. Siberia*, anchored some distance from shore, and began decanting its passengers onto the larger ship—a reasonably respectable, well-dressed lot by the look of them. One by one they went aboard the larger vessel, moved along the deck, and disappeared into the ship's innards. Stewards followed carrying the passengers' luggage, which consisted of an astonishing number of boxes, trunks, suitcases, baskets, hatboxes, and crates. Of these Americans headed back to the states, some had arrived in Yokohama six weeks earlier, while others had first set foot on Japanese soil four months ago. The principal part of what they were taking home was not visible: for the rest of their lives, they would be able to conjure up visions of what they'd seen and done since their arrival in the Far East.

Mabel Boardman could recall a slog through a Mindanao jungle.

Thirteen-year-old Roland Harriman would always wonder why he'd not fallen ill with a dreadful disease in Peking.

Amy McMillan could look back on an unforgettable afternoon on the deck of a battleship in the Yellow Sea.

Cal McKnight would never forget a furious mob in a Tokyo street.

Nick Longworth could recollect a courtship conducted under the vigilant eyes of the secretary of war and a clutch of congressional wives.

Young Mary Harriman would cherish the memory of meeting, in an unlikely place, a man she could finally care about.

Edith Newlands would remember the challenges of being Alice Roosevelt's chaperone.

Congressman Driscoll would never forget how his shoes squeaked as he strode forward to be introduced to Japan's Emperor Mitsuhito.

Dr. Lyle could savor the knowledge that he'd come in first in a marksmanship contest against Japanese soldiers.

Alice Roosevelt would forever hear "Banzai!" ringing in her mind.

And Edward Henry Harriman had, in his pocket, a piece of paper he'd traveled halfway around the world to obtain.

PART II

STARTING SOMETHING

Winter 1903 to June 1905

1

Boston: Unwelcome Letter

In a fury, Alice snatched up the letter and set a match to it.[1]

She should have known there would be consequences. On a delightful summer day, she and Ellen "Lila" Paul had sped in Lila's motorcar from Newport to Boston at the dizzying pace of thirty-miles-an-hour. They'd visited friends in Newport and then headed for the home of Alice's grandfather, Lee, where Alice would make her much-anticipated annual weeklong summer visit.[2]

As they drove and the road rolled out in front of them, breezes ruffled their hair and sweet summer smells intrigued their senses. The girls had been exhilarated with the realization that the car held just the two of them; no older married woman accompanied them. They were chaperone-free! For the moment, it was glorious!

Because Alice was the daughter of the president and drew national attention everywhere she went, their journey was soon reported in the newspapers.[3] It reminded her of the time, a while back, when she was traveling with Emily Spinach, her pet snake. "I named it Emily after a very thin aunt, and 'spinach' because it was green," she said. "I tucked it into a stocking box because it was a garter snake . . . the stories multiplied about Emily Spinach and you would have thought I was harboring a boa constrictor. Friends wouldn't allow me in their homes with it."[4]

In a group picture of proper young ladies, Alice would have been the one out of focus. When she was a youngster, her family called her a "guttersnipe" because she was the only girl in a boys' club.[5] By the time she was twenty-one, she was living as much by her own rules as she could manage. Alice smoked cigarettes. Her parents told her she could absolutely not smoke under their roof . . . and so Alice simply marched up three flights of stairs to smoke *on top* of their roof, which happened to be the roof of the White House. "I smoked on the roof, outdoors, and in everyone else's house," she would later recall. "I . . . naturally smoked to annoy the family."[6]

In the early part of the twentieth century, marriage was the expected career for a young woman. Because appearances were everything, a well-brought-up young woman was expected to have a chaperone accompany her when she traveled, and she was not supposed to spend time alone with a man unless they were engaged. And it was generally thought unseemly for a woman to drive a motorcar.[7]

The report that the president's daughter had driven from Newport to Boston without a chaperone was headline news, and Theodore Roosevelt could read the headlines as well as anyone else. He fired off a blistering letter to his daughter, and before she opened it, she may have hoped that her father had written that he missed her and wished she were at home with the family. When she slit open the envelope, what she found was a letter that, as she put it, "scorched the paper it was written on."[8]

Her father enumerated her most recent departures from what he and her stepmother believed proper for a well-brought-up young lady. He told her she seemed to lack any sign of affection for her nearest and dearest, put her own pleasure foremost, and didn't even care enough to write. He asserted that she was simply courting publicity.[9]

The latter was what stung the most, and Alice was indignant. "There he was, one of the greatest experts in publicity there ever was," she explained to a friend later in life, "accusing me of trying to steal the spotlight!"[10]

She could recall with satisfaction her success at her father's public functions: helping her stepmother receive guests at White House events, where she greeted her parents' guests with a warm, welcoming manner and thoughtful conversation.[11]

But praise from acquaintances is not the same as praise from loved ones. The very same girl who received these accolades had once told her stepmother, Edith: "Father doesn't care for me, that is to say, one eighth as much as he does for the other children." She went on: "Of course he loves me in a way because I am one of his children, and he certainly does have his much-prized sense of duty." She confided to Edith that she really did love her father with all the love that she was capable of.[12]

For now, she would do what she had to do: she sat down and wrote the obligatory "I promise to do better" letter to her father. Although what she craved was her father's admiration, at least she had his attention.

By this time (she was nineteen), Alice felt like a pathetic, homely creature, and thought that people only admired her and said she was pretty because she was the president's daughter. So she made the decision not to be a "pathetic creature." Instead, she would be resistant and contrary. To herself, she vowed to become "conspicuous." She would forego the role of dutiful, tractable daughter and chart her own course.[13]

Meanwhile, there was the letter, its very existence reproaching her. She burned it and watched as the flame turned it to ashes.

2

New York: Invitation Extended

Edward Henry Harriman was "starting something," which is what he did when he had an idea but didn't know where it was going.[14] His mind spanned a continent, and now it was vaulting across the Pacific Ocean, speculating about opportunities there for a railroad (and shipping) man in the Far East. As always, he was thinking decades ahead of anyone else—although he had no clear vision, much less a clear plan of how he could make that vision a reality. But when he learned that the new U.S. minister to Japan, Lloyd Griscom, would be passing through New York, the Harrimans invited Griscom and his wife, Elsa, to dinner.

Elsa Griscom knew Edward's daughter, Mary Harriman, but neither she nor her husband had met Mary's parents.[15] "Why would this man we've never met want to entertain us?" they must have wondered.

Wrapped in the winter's chill, the young couple knocked and waited on the doorstep of the Harrimans' handsome townhouse. Damp from the East River mingled with the cold that bounced off facades of stone and concrete. The result was a winter's evening that was uniquely New York. When their hosts opened the door to welcome their guests, it was the warmth pouring out that enveloped and pulled the couple forward into the foyer.

After introductions, the evening began comfortably. Conversation flowed, helped by Elsa Griscom's acquaintance with young Mary.[16] The

Griscoms certainly knew Edward Harriman by reputation—his railroad acquisitions often made the front page—but until now, Lloyd and Elsa had never met the man face-to-face.[17] The son of an Episcopal minister whose salary barely supported his family,[18] E. H. Harriman had grown up to become a legend, known to some as the "human business machine." He'd tangled with Wall Street's mighty J. P. Morgan and won,[19] he'd taken over an undervalued, bankrupt Union Pacific Railroad and made it profitable,[20] and he'd acquired control over the Southern Pacific Railroad and its subsidiary, the Pacific Mail Steamship Line.[21] Challenges nourished him, and he thought it might be time for a new one. Talking with Lloyd Griscom would give him insight into a part of the world that had only since the end of the Spanish-American War come into American consciousness: the Far East. The Far East looked, to Harriman, to be a part of the world ripe for expanding U.S. interests.[22]

As the highest-ranking U.S. diplomat assigned to Japan, Lloyd Griscom was delighted to find himself headed for Tokyo, a place where something important might actually happen, unlike his previous post in Tehran.[23] There, absolutely nothing ever occurred that would interest anyone outside the country's borders. In the Far East, business was beginning to percolate, and one of Griscom's responsibilities would be the promotion of U.S. commercial interests there. He couldn't know how complicated his duties would become.

The evening went well. After dinner, Harriman was happy to explain to Griscom how he'd transformed the hapless Union Pacific into a thriving, well-managed, and profitable operation: he'd reduced grades and straightened curves while upgrading rolling stock, so trains could carry heavier loads and more quickly reach their destinations.[24] "Efficiency, efficiency, efficiency" was his mantra, one that he'd enforced at every opportunity. Railroads were essential to the nation's expanding industrial machine, and Harriman's control over one of the nation's largest networks made him a very powerful man. Harriman was to railroads as

Carnegie was to steel and Rockefeller to oil.[25]

Harriman quizzed Griscom on opportunities for business in Japan while Griscom, for his part, tried to take the measure of this surprisingly short man. At only five feet and four inches tall,[26] Harriman sported an outsize bushy mustache, possibly to distract attention from his thinning hair. It was difficult to reconcile this quiet, relaxed man with the newspapers' depiction of him as a ruthless manipulator. He'd bought a seat on the New York Stock Exchange when he was twenty-one, and now, in his fifties, he controlled a transcontinental railroad network, and more.

Only recently, the Griscoms had spent a weekend at the White House as guests of President and Mrs. Theodore Roosevelt, and now Griscom was struck by the contrast between the president and Harriman. Roosevelt, Griscom thought, was energetic, direct, and powerful,[27] and he relished being at the center of every stage. As Alice Roosevelt would later put it, "He wanted to be the bride at every wedding and the corpse at every funeral."[28]

Harriman, on the other hand, was, as Griscom said in his memoirs, "the very antithesis of the president . . . a quiet, rarely smiling man who spoke in a soft voice, with no striding into the room, no pounding the table for emphasis, no coining of phrases, no quality of being picturesque."[29] But Griscom realized that Harriman, in his undramatic way, was every bit as dynamic a personality as Roosevelt in his analysis of problems and how to solve them.[30] Each man was as forceful and focused as a derecho wind.

As the dinner party ended and they said their goodbyes, Griscom remarked casually, "You ought to see what's at the end of your steamship line. Why not come out to Tokyo and visit us?"

Without a pause, Harriman shot back. "You may be getting more than you bargained for," he warned. "It sounds like a good idea to me."[31]

How things would work out, he didn't know, but E. H. Harriman had indeed started something.

3
Tokyo: War's Onset

Lloyd Griscom needed to establish common ground with the person sitting across from him. The man's frame was thin, and his sharp eyes and quick movements indicated extraordinary vigor. Jutaro Komura was Japan's foreign minister. His help was essential for Griscom to make headway with Japanese-American trade issues, such as Japanese restrictions on American insurance firms that prevented them from making a profit in Japan. Knowing that Komura was a graduate of Harvard's law school, Griscom ventured a comment about the university. After a moment Komura smiled, and a relaxed give-and-take about Harvard followed. Griscom seized the opportunity to bring up the trade restriction problem.[32]

As soon as Griscom began to talk about trade restrictions, Komura's face closed up, as if someone had slammed down the shutter at a ticket seller's window. Griscom realized that Komura was simply not going to discuss the subject of trade. He thought that it was difficult to get any idea of what Japanese officials were even thinking, such was the invisible barrier with which they surrounded themselves.

He also suspected that the Japanese felt slighted that the U.S. had sent such a young representative to their country. Japanese diplomats tended to be much older than he, and he knew they thought him too young for the job.[33] Since he couldn't do much about the age difference, he would have to persist and hope for some sort of breakthrough.

As different as it was from their home in the U.S., the Griscoms' quarters in Tokyo were an oasis of comfort compared to the rigors of their previous post in Persia. There they'd suffered from excessive damp and dirt and a lack of water and heat, and only had a tin box for an oven. When they'd arrived in Japan's capital in June of 1903, they'd caught their first glimpse of the U.S. legation grounds through an arch of bright pink plum and cherry blossoms. Their quarters turned out to be an undistinguished but comfortable white frame house, easily updated by the plumbing fixtures and wallpaper they'd had the foresight to bring with them.[34]

Next door to the U.S. legation lived Hirobumi Ito, one of the *genro*, a group of elder statesmen and former samurai who'd brought European military, financial, educational, and industrial experts to Japan to train the upcoming generation in modern ways. Ito had been Japan's prime minister and was internationally respected. Because he had put aside his country's traditional discomfort with foreigners, Ito and Griscom were able to chat comfortably in their adjoining gardens.[35]

Ito and Griscom became friends, but in other instances, bridging the cultural divide had taxed the Griscoms' flexibility. Once, early on in their residency, they were preparing to entertain one of the elder statesmen. An hour before the guests were scheduled to appear, the couple were still shifting furniture and putting the final touches on the flowers, not yet dressed for the party. To their astonishment and dismay, Count Matsukata, the guest of honor, was suddenly ushered in, obviously prepared to stay. Elsa could excuse herself to dress, but etiquette required that Griscom sit with their guest until one of the other legation officials appeared. As the Griscoms later learned, Count Matsukata believed that his early arrival showed respect for his hosts.[36]

Another gathering—this time in honor of Prince and Princess Kanin—turned out to be their most embarrassing. They'd labored mightily on their white-themed party, anxious to make a graceful splash as new and young members of Tokyo's diplomatic corps. The legation had never looked so bright and cheerful. Hundreds of white lanterns glittered like fairy lights from every possible spot on the legation grounds. Indoors, moss and ferns from Kyoto formed the background for the striking table arrangement of white camellias.

Their guests appeared to enjoy themselves, and the Griscoms felt the party had been a success. "When the last guest had stepped into his carriage, we went to bed feeling distinctly puffed up."[37] Until several days later, that is, when an imperial chamberlain paid Griscom a call on behalf of the Japanese officials to thank him for the party. After a few minutes of polite conversation, the chamberlain mentioned that they had been puzzled by the decorations.

"Perhaps you do not know, Your Excellency, that among our people white is the color for funerals," explained the chamberlain.

Years later, in his memoirs, Griscom recalled, "We were the laughingstock of the diplomatic corps and were properly deflated."[38]

Frustrations and gaffes aside, Griscom was excited to be in a place where American prestige was increasing, and which promised to be the scene of meaningful action. He was right about the action—more than he knew—and right about Japan's increasing importance in the world.

By September 1903, tensions were growing between Japan and Russia. Russia had increased its presence in Manchuria and was expanding its presence in Korea. China had once had control of Korea, but following a war with Japan in 1894 in which Japan was the victor, China was forced to cede that right to Japan. The same peace treaty also required China to pay an indemnity to Japan, for which China had to borrow money and turn to Russia to guarantee the loans. In exchange, Russia secured the rights to build railways and telephone lines in Manchuria, as well as the right to berth part of its navy in the harbor at Port Arthur on Manchuria's southern tip. Alarm bells rang for the Japanese as they saw the Russian naval presence and Russian troops grow in Manchuria. More and more Russians seemed to appear in Korea, and the Japanese came to believe that the Russians had their eyes on Korea as well.

Japanese governing officials felt that Korea was essential as a source of food to nourish Japan's growing population and were anxious to achieve an agreement with the Russians. Consequently, over several months, Japanese diplomats made various proposals about neutral zones, rights, concessions, and paramount interests, all with little or no response from the Russians. Hirobumi Ito, Griscom's neighbor, traveled to Moscow in an attempt to persuade the Russian government to agree to separate spheres of influence: Japan in Korea and Russia in Manchuria. Russia's minister of finance, Count Sergei Witte, was agreeable but unable to persuade others who had the tsar's ear. Many in the Russian government thought that Russia could treat Japan as a bear would flick a bee away from a honey hive.[39] But all of that was about to change.

On February 6, 1904, the Japanese foreign minister summoned Griscom to his office. Baron Komura was alone, and when Griscom entered, the baron sprang up. "The Japanese government has reached the end of its patience," he said. "We are recalling our minister from St. Petersburg. Baron Rosen [the Russian ambassador to Japan] will be handed his passports."

Griscom stared at Baron Komura. "That means war, Your Excellency."

"We have no choice," was Komura's reply.

"Will the Japanese armies act without a formal declaration?" Griscom asked.

"Absolutely not!" the baron replied.[40]

On February 9, 1904, without a declaration of war, the Japanese fleet surprised the commanders of Russian naval vessels in Port Arthur, Manchuria, with a devastating attack. At the same time, near Korea's port of Chemulpo, ships of the Japanese fleet opened fire on the Russian warships *Variag* and *Koriets*. Russia's ships sank to the bottom of the sea before their captains could fully grasp what was happening. When the surprise attack was over, Japan controlled the sea between the disputed parts of the mainland and its home islands.[41] On February 11, Japan officially declared war, initiating hostilities that, due to the sheer number of casualties on both sides, captured much of the world's attention. By the time the war ended, Japan would no longer be a small island nation.

And because the Japanese government was anxious to have U.S. support in its dispute with Russia, Griscom was surprised to find all his demands for solutions to U.S.-Japanese trade problems eagerly granted.[42]

4
Tokyo: Painful Parting

Lloyd Griscom was not looking forward to saying farewell to the Russian ambassador Roman Rovanovich Rosen and his wife, but as a member of Tokyo's diplomatic corps, he knew he had to. But he stopped first at the British ministry to see if Sir Claude MacDonald would accompany him—the unflappable Colonel Sir Claude Maxwell MacDonald would be a reassuring companion for this tense social situation.

Unfortunately, Sir Claude was out, but Second Secretary Thomas Hohler was in. "How about our going to the Rosens' together?" Griscom suggested. "They can't do more than throw us out."

When they entered the drawing room in the home of the Russian minister and his wife, they saw their fellow diplomats clustered in uneasy groups, clutching teacups and uttering chopped sentences in subdued voices. The gathering felt like a funeral visitation for an almost-but-not-quite respectable citizen: nobody knew quite what to say. Now that the Japanese navy had successfully executed a surprise attack on the Russian fleet, destroying two warships outside Chemulpo and bottling up the remainder in the harbor at Port Arthur, the diplomats knew war had already begun. The Japanese had handed Baron and Baroness Rosen their passports and asked them to leave.

Rosen was well liked and had served as Russia's voice in Tokyo for several years. He had friends of many nationalities in Tokyo's close-knit diplomatic corps, and now many of them struggled with feelings of sadness. Because those in the room were sympathetic to the Japanese cause, they had mixed feelings. "For the Rosens," Griscom said later, "it was a personal tragedy. The members of the corps who had once been their friends now remembered that the Rosens were Russians, and in this affair deserved no sympathy."[43]

Seeing Baron and Baroness Rosen standing together, Griscom and Hohler moved to speak to them. When they expressed their regrets at his departure, the baron accepted stoically; as they turned to speak to the baroness, she erupted like a pent-up volcano, her raised, shrill voice reaching every person in the room.

"How dare you pretend to be our friends while you were knifing us in the back all this time?"

The silence that followed was thick and uncomfortable, and broken only when the baron cleared his throat and asked, "Would anyone care for more tea?"

"Yes," they murmured and moved toward the tea table to fill their cups, heads down despite knowing they had done nothing underhanded.

"We gulped it down and departed as soon as possible," Griscom noted.

When they were safely in their carriage, Hohler mumbled, "Thank God that's over"—a sentiment Griscom shared.[44]

So Griscom said goodbye to two Russian friends. But he was about to greet hundreds of Americans the war would lure to the Far East.

5

Peking: Career Change

Swinging incense burners, priests led the way for a slight, unimpressive figure wearing a dark-colored silky coat and an ordinary official's hat with a crimson button. The group crossed the courtyard of the Buddhist temple at Yung Ho Kung to the yard's center, where a sedan chair waited, resplendent in golden silk, gold fittings, and yellow shafts. Shaft bearers in spiked helmets stood guard over its magnificence. Members of the imperial bodyguard, armed with huge swords in green scabbards, milled about amongst rotund eunuchs and uniformed officials. Buddhist monks watched from a distance. Then the silk-clad figure, eyes on the ground, strode toward the chair as the priests accompanying him dropped to their knees. In short order, the shaft bearers knelt, the silk-clad figure sat in the chair, the bodyguard formed around him, standard bearers carrying imperial yellow banners brought up the rear, and the procession moved smartly out of the courtyard. The emperor of China was departing. As the ensemble left through a side gate, bugles sounded, and priests, monks, and officials jumbled together to follow the emperor.[45]

A line of monks draped in grubby purple lama robes broke away from the crowd and shuffled toward the nearby lamasery. Without a sound, the tallest of them dropped out and quickly made his way into one of the nearest monk's quarters. A few minutes passed. Then, Willard Straight emerged. He had been transformed from a purple-robed monk into a tall Westerner, clad in trousers, stiff-collared shirt, necktie, and jacket.

An unwelcome outsider who was simply curious about the emperor, Straight had spent the past twenty-four hours hiding in the lamasery, part of it under the temple altar, just to watch Emperor Guangxu at his devotions. Now, Straight needed to get back to his regular occupation as assistant to the head of the Chinese Customs Service.

His mind nearly burst with images of what he'd seen as the emperor underwent a ceremonial purification in the hour just after dawn: the temple's great courtyard lit by enormous silken lanterns; priests' heads topped with yellow lacquer hats; officiants bearing golden censers; lamas in yellow silks, their shoulders draped with red scarves; and over it all, the pervasive smell of incense. Eight priests had chanted as the emperor stood before one altar, then moved to another altar, followed by men carrying large packages wrapped in yellow silk (gifts from the emperor to the lamasery). And in the midst of the fanfare, Straight was taken aback by the thought that this young, delicate-looking man was the nominal ruler of four hundred million people.[46]

Such exotic sights brightened the young American's days in China, but after a time, Straight realized that he was not happy with his situation. As he saw it, he had two choices: he could continue his work as assistant to the head of the Chinese Customs Service and likely be promoted to a position of more responsibility; or he could follow his artistic talent for sketching portraits down a very different path.

The more he thought about it, the more he knew that neither option alone would satisfy his longing for a creative and important enterprise. Collins of Reuters News Service had recently offered him a job as a correspondent in Korea. Would this offer lead in the direction he wanted to go?

After two years with the Chinese Customs Service, he had become distressingly aware that he was bored—not with China, but with the bureaucratic life. For a while, learning the language and customs of China had provided an exciting challenge (six months just to learn 219 characters and then several more months to learn the various inflections necessary to convey meaning), but now that was done.[47] He needed more challenges.

Straight didn't know what he wanted to do, but he knew he wanted to do it in the Far East. When he was only eight, his widowed mother had taken a position as a teacher in a girls' school in Tokyo, and they lived in a house on university grounds. His mother was thoroughly occupied with her work, which gave young Willard an opportunity to range forth and explore. His ingenious pranks gave him a reputation out of proportion to his years—his mother was regularly interrupted at work by messengers reporting her young son's presence in some unlikely or forbidden place. His imagination expressed itself in bizarre activities, which surprised Willard as much as they disconcerted his family.[48]

Tokyo's sights impressed themselves upon him, and young Willard started to draw some of what he saw. His mother saw his sketches and arranged for him to have lessons from a Japanese artist.[49] Thus began a lifelong habit of sketching the people he encountered.

Now in Peking, his curiosity and interest drew him into the streets where he experienced odiferous camel trains, donkeys and their jingling bells, street vendors crying their wares, and skin-draped Mongols intoning their prayers. He sketched the people he saw: a river coolie; a courtier; an off-duty soldier; lamas; laborers; a boatman; and even one of the educated class, or literati. Within the compound where he lived, Straight sketched his friends and Western reporters who stopped in Peking. He had a gift for capturing the essence of a person and could have made a living with his art. But he didn't see himself as a "society artist," doing portraits for a living.

The Boxer Rebellion had ended only the year before he arrived, and as Straight wrote to a friend, he felt that Peking's legation quarter was a fortress.[50] He and the other residents of the quarter had to rely on themselves for entertainment—he sang with a close harmony group, acted in plays, and wrote, produced, and acted in original song and dance skits. Before long, Straight was a welcome guest at dinner tables in the international community. There he heard tales of international intrigue, including stories about Peking's many foreign nationals during the Boxer rebellion, trapped there by Chinese people who were angry at foreigners' exploitation of their country.[51]

Straight socialized with the American and British reporters who frequently passed through Peking and stayed in the diplomatic compound. By the end of 1903, they regularly brought rumors of a possible war between Japan and Russia. Over this time, he met Robert Moore Collins, a correspondent for Reuters who one day asked Straight, "How about working for Reuters as a correspondent in Korea?"[52]

Straight was not trained as a reporter—he had a degree in architecture from Cornell—and wasn't sure if the work would lead to anything. He temporized.

Three months later, the Japanese attacked Port Arthur and declared war on Russia.

Collins repeated his offer. He wanted Straight to report to Nagasaki, Japan, immediately.

Within a few days, Straight left the customs service behind. He was about to become a war correspondent.

6
Tokyo: Restive Reporter

As U.S. minister, part of Lloyd Griscom's job was to look after the interests of U.S. citizens in Japan. As the flames of war between Japan and Russia grew, a plethora of American reporters and correspondents descended on Tokyo, planning to go immediately to Manchuria to begin filing war stories.

To their intense frustration, they'd learned that the men who ran the Japanese government and commanded the army felt no need to please an inquisitive batch of reporters whose stories they would never read. They refused to give permission for reporters to travel anywhere near the battlefields.

"Do something!" the correspondents beseeched Griscom. He pleaded in vain with the Japanese authorities, saying that the correspondents had come halfway around the world so that they could inform the American public about the war. The war was not being fought in Tokyo, and to write meaningful stories, these men needed to be where the two armies were fighting . . . in Manchuria.

"I explained to Baron Komura that these fellow countrymen of mine represented the leading American papers, that upon their reports depended American public opinion, and that nobody had ever tried to keep war correspondents away from the front lines," Griscom said. "But the authorities were unyielding."[53]

The reporters started to trickle into Tokyo early in 1904, just as hostilities began. Others followed in a steady stream. Months later, they were all still in Tokyo. Many were freelancers, hoping to score a headline-grabbing story. Others were accredited by established news organizations: the Hearst papers; the Associated Press (A.P.); and Reuters.

Martin Egan, the personable correspondent of the Associated Press, pulled ahead of the pack by cultivating contacts in all departments of Japanese government, not just those connected with the war. Egan spread a wide net. He was on good terms with business leaders and with the *genro*, Japan's elder statesmen.

A popular speaker, Egan was invited everywhere, and he liked to entertain his journalist friends in his charming cottage. Willard Straight was one of those who enjoyed listening to Egan—who often told his stories stretched out on a divan with a cigar in his mouth—expand on his experiences working in New York or covering the Spanish-American War in the Philippines. Others of the correspondents' cadre, among them Collins of Reuters, Palmer of *Collier's* magazine, and Bass of *The Chicago Herald*, added tales of the wider world, Japanese politics, and military and naval affairs.[54]

They were men who'd experienced at close hand the stories they'd reported on. Having come halfway around the world to write about the current war and its battles, they were frustrated with their inability to report colorful stories from the front lines. Japanese suspicion of foreigners persisted when it came to protecting their military operations from the eyes of outsiders. Whenever the journalists applied for papers that would allow them into places where battles were likely to take place, they were put off with excuses.[55]

Not that the life they were leading was oppressive; most of them were quartered in the Imperial Hotel, across from Hibiya Park and next to the home minister's property. The spacious hotel had been built to cater to Western visitors so that guests did not have to dine on the floor or take off their shoes in Japanese tradition. The many reporters used the hotel's lobby and lounge as if it were a not-very-discriminating club. The aroma of tobacco filled the space, and a miasma of blue smoke from their pipes and cigarettes hovered like a Newfoundland fog. The government, anxious to distract these inquiring minds, arranged frequent dinners and outings. The Griscoms entertained them. The reporters entertained each other. Despite their frustrations, these men lived days full of pleasant comfort.[56]

One day, however, one of their number went missing. Jack London had gone south.[57] London was more a novelist than a reporter, but he had a gift for colorful descriptions of what he saw. Now with credentials from Hearst, by heaven, he was going to get them a story, permission or no permission. He was determined to find a way to get himself and his camera to Korea and Manchuria.

He'd arrived aboard the *Siberia* from San Francisco with another writer and adventurer, Richard Harding Davis. On the leisurely voyage across the Pacific, the two had become fast friends.[58] Davis had covered both the Boer and Spanish-American wars and was a playwright and author of books about his adventures. His good looks and impeccable manners made him a welcome guest in anything from mansions to grass huts, and he had become friends with Theodore Roosevelt in Cuba when Roosevelt and his Rough Riders had thrust themselves into the Spanish-American War.[59]

That friendship was going to be extremely important to his new friend, Jack London. The product of a hard-scrabble life, Jack London was as rough as Davis was polished. At fourteen, London had left home on his own, and had since lived as a sailor, a hobo, an Alaska prospector and, eventually, a writer of adventure stories like *The Sea Wolf*, finished only the year before.[60] In Tokyo, he relished the good life and camaraderie at the Imperial Hotel, but all his life he'd been accustomed to independent action. Eventually, he made his move.[61]

After London left his fellow reporters exchanging tall tales in Tokyo, he made his way south to Kobe and then to Nagasaki, where he scoured the waterfront for passage to Korea. No luck. Finally, when he reached Moji at the western end of the Inland Sea, he found a ship headed for Chemulpo, the port for Seoul, Korea. Before boarding, he snapped pictures of the local scene in Moji to send to his stateside editors. What London didn't realize was that Moji was a fortified city, an embarkation point for troops headed to Korea, and foreigners were absolutely forbidden to take pictures. He was arrested and the police confiscated his camera.[62]

London wired Richard Harding Davis with a plea for help; Davis went immediately to Lloyd Griscom. Davis and Griscom knew each other well—they had survived heat, humidity, insects, and fevers when they slogged through the Nicaraguan jungle together from Atlantic to Pacific years before. Griscom took the case to Baron Komura, the foreign minister. By this time London had been tried, fined, and released, but the authorities still held his camera.

Despite Griscom's pleas, Komura supported the authorities. He and his legal counsel explained that the weapon with which a crime has been committed becomes the property of the court, and there was no way around that.

Griscom, a lawyer himself, thought a moment, and then asked, "Does that apply to every crime?"

"Every crime of every description," Komura replied.

Griscom straightened up. "If I can name a crime to which it does not apply," he posed, "will you release the camera?"

After a moment, Komura agreed.

"Well, what about rape?"

After a moment of thought, even the cautious diplomat had to admit defeat.[63]

The story made the rounds, and Jack London got his camera back. He immediately returned to making his way to the war. He found passage to

Pusan, Korea, where he boarded another coaster headed for Chemulpo, but the Japanese military seized the boat and put London and his fellow passengers ashore.

London pondered. With his sailing experience, he could buy a boat and sail himself to Chemulpo. Why not? He'd hire a crew with some local knowledge, and they could work their way along the western coast of Korea.

In the middle of February, London sailed his boat through gale-force winds, blinding snow, and freezing spray, until he finally sighted the harbor at Chemulpo. Once ashore, he found himself in wretched condition, his hands and feet frostbitten.

London recovered and reported on a part of the war where Russian Cossack cavalry reconnoitered two-hundred miles into Japanese-held territory. He documented the Japanese march north into Manchuria and sent his stories and pictures back to the U.S. to appear in the Hearst papers.

After another trespassing infraction in Manchuria, he was arrested once again by the Japanese military authorities. After his release, he found himself face-to-face with a Japanese soldier stealing fodder from his horse. London was furious. Without a thought, he pulled his arm back and felt his fist pound into the soldier's face. "It was the most satisfying punch I ever delivered," he said.

This was serious. A military court and a possible death penalty loomed. Once more he wired Richard Harding Davis. Davis asked one of London's fans to intervene: Theodore Roosevelt. Roosevelt wielded his presidential powers, and London was released on the condition that he depart Korea immediately. When London finally left for the States he had, by some accounts, filed more stories than any other correspondent.[64]

Richard Harding Davis was in one of the first groups of reporters that military officials finally permitted to go to Manchuria. But he never got closer than eight miles from a battle, and when he returned to Tokyo, he threw up his hands and decided to head for the States.[65]

The land war stalemated, and Griscom enjoyed a temporary respite before trying circumstances would complicate his next role: host extraordinaire.

7
Washington: Anxious Romance

"No young woman could ever be more frivolous, inane, more scattered than I was," Alice Roosevelt recalled in her memoirs twenty-eight years later.[66] At twenty-one, she was partly preoccupied with having fun while another part of her agonized about her relationship with Nick Longworth, the current man in her life. Were they engaged or not? Each time they had a spat (and there were many), she wondered, "Would he come back?"

Nick was interesting. He was thirty-six, and she liked older men. He played the violin and the piano, and he sang. He could compose witty lyrics on the spot.[67] Plus, Alice already had a taste for politics, and Nick was a U.S. congressman.

But experience had taught Alice that people important to her couldn't always be counted on to be present. Her mother had died immediately after she was born, and her father was totally absent until she was three. Once her father remarried, the adoring aunt who raised Alice handed her over to her new stepmother, who did her conscientious best but was still reserved and distant.[68] Alice was wary of expecting too much of relationships. Still, she yearned for one that would lead to marriage.

Alice's unease about Nick was not solely due to her own insecurities. Even though he had been pursuing Alice since Christmas, Nick's reputation as a womanizer included hints of several long-term liaisons.[69]

Soon she was expected to make a late-spring trip to Cincinnati to meet his family, whose money had allowed Nick to plunge into politics as a diversion, not a vocation.

Even before Nick was elected to congress, Alice was lighting up the Washington scene. The assassination of William McKinley had catapulted her father into the presidency and sixteen-year-old Alice into the limelight.

"I was brought up on the principle that 'nice' people didn't get their names in the papers except when they were born, when they were married, or when they died," she commented to a friend many years later. Nevertheless, the name of the president's daughter graced the pages of the nation's newspapers often enough to exasperate her father.[70]

She didn't set out to be a celebrity. As the first young woman in the White House since Nellie Grant (President Ulysses S. Grant's daughter) left in 1877, Alice was a magnet for reporters and photographers.[71] Not a "Polly-sit-by-the fire," she was out and about, doing unconventional things like carrying a pet snake or traveling without a chaperone. There were rumors that she'd been asked to leave the Copley Plaza Hotel in Boston because she was found smoking in the lobby.[72] And a photographer had once captured her paying money to a bookie at the races.[73]

Alice and her father had yet another point of friction between them: her friends. Theodore Roosevelt wondered why she couldn't spend more time with her cousin Eleanor, who chose to volunteer at a settlement house in New York's Lower East Side.[74] Alice, it seemed, preferred to gad about with the offspring of New York's high society or with titled European diplomats in Washington.

One of her friends, Countess Marguerite "Maggie" Cassini, was daughter of the Russian ambassador and two years older than Alice. Maggie added another level to Alice's tower of insecurities about Nick and about herself. The year Alice turned twenty, the two girls had formed a tight little circle with Charlie de Chambrun and Nick Longworth. The four spent hours together, taking in dinners, dances, taffy-pulls, sleigh rides, and skating parties. They were not paired off, but Alice began to fancy herself in love with Charlie. Maggie Cassini had discovered that she enjoyed trying to provoke her friends by playing up to their beaux. She was experienced in the art of flirtation and soon had Charlie writing her passionate love letters. Alice could recognize when a door had been slammed in her face. She decided to turn her attentions to Nick Longworth. He'd always given Alice lots of attention, but he'd been smitten with Maggie since they first met, when she'd been introduced to him as someone "very dangerous."[75]

Always careful to keep her voice light and casual, Alice would regularly ask Maggie if Nick had proposed yet, and Maggie, with a toss of her head, would say that he hadn't. One day, the two girls were up on the roof of the White House, smoking. They could see the Washington Monument and hear the sounds of anonymous comings and goings in the grounds below. Alice made her customary inquiry: "Has Nick proposed to you?"

"Yes," Maggie answered. Alice felt as though a millstone had fallen on her. Nick had asked Maggie to marry him. Maggie turned him down, but Alice grieved in her journal that she had set her heart first on Charley de Chambrun and then on Nick Longworth, and Maggie had wrested them both away from her. Why, Alice lamented to her journal, was she "such a pill?"[76]

That was the end of that friendship. Within the year, Maggie's father was recalled to St. Petersburg, and Maggie Cassini was out of Washington.

Meanwhile, Alice's escapades continued to distract her father, so he put her to work. She cut ribbons at official functions and was even the star of a boat christening. She was invited to christen the yacht that the German Kaiser had built on Shooter's Island in New York Bay. That February in New York City was the coldest on record,[77] but Alice effectively smashed the bottle of champagne into the ship's bow, intoning the traditional, "In the name of His Majesty, the German Emperor, I christen this yacht 'Meteor!'" Of the event, she wrote that Prince Henry of Prussia "gave me a bunch of pink roses, congratulated me and kissed my hand and we all trooped over to a lunch given by the shipbuilding people."[78]

Alice had proved herself capable of representing her popular father. But for Theodore Roosevelt, what to do about Alice was an ongoing problem.

Now it was March 4, 1905. Alice had just seen her father inaugurated as president of the United States—his first full term—and was in the reviewing stand, waving at friends and trying to watch the inaugural parade while she simultaneously clutched at her white, dishpan-sized hat. The fluffy ostrich plumes on top whipped about wildly, and the wind ducked under the hat's black-lined brim and threatened to lift the concoction off her head and send it sailing into the crowd. "It was a sparkling, windy March day, the stand was in the open . . . and to keep that hat on at the proper angle was almost more trouble than it was worth," Alice declared.

The parade marched on. Bands followed one another, and flags flew all about. Alice's young sister, Ethel, and one of her brothers buzzed around like worker bees, taking pictures.

For the benefit of out-of-towners, the inaugural committee had labeled historic buildings and the homes of people of public interest. Alice was inspired. She had a friend's valet produce a set of signs for the homes of friends, identical to the official ones. On these they inscribed clever characterizations, such as for New York congressman Bourke Cockran, who was a professional Irish sympathizer: "Here lives the Irish Ambassador. All he needs is an embassy."

When the signs were ready, however, one of her co-conspirators lost his nerve and wouldn't agree to putting them up. "We did, however, use the one we had made for Nick. It read, quite simply, 'I live here. Nicholas Longworth.' We kept it on the house for some time and maneuvered Nick to stand in the window over it, unconscious it was there, while sightseeing stages passed, looked, and then shouted with laughter."[79]

Alice definitely had Nick's attention, but could she keep it?

8

Washington: Offer Accepted

By the spring of 1905, the war between Japan and Russia was more than a year old and had resulted in hundreds of thousands of casualties on each side. The president's diplomatic sources told him that both countries' resources were stretched so thin, they might be persuaded to come to the negotiating table.[80]

If Theodore Roosevelt had known when he volunteered his services as a peace mediator in the Far East that he'd be dealing with, as he put it, "shiftiness, corruption, mendacity, and just plain incompetence," he might have reconsidered.[81] Then again, his anxiety over the balance of power in the Far East might yet have propelled him into action.[82] Since its acquisition of the Philippines at the end of the Spanish-American War, the U.S. had its own Far Eastern interests and wanted stability in the region. For this reason, the president was anxious for peace. He was also anxious about Japan's postwar intentions toward its neighbors.

Because Secretary of State John Hay was seriously ill and out of the country, Theodore Roosevelt was acting as his own secretary of state. From the first, he found that bringing Japan and Russia face-to-face across a negotiating table was a challenge.[83] Each side felt that being the first to agree to initiate a peace process would indicate weakness. The Japanese were being coy and the Russians just plain difficult; Japanese foreign minister Jutaro Komura told Lloyd Griscom that his government had discussed peace terms but wouldn't disclose them until some overture for peace had come from the Russian government,[84] while Count Cassini, Russian ambassador to the U.S., mourned, "We are condemned to fight. We cannot honestly stop."[85] But it could be worth it: to bring about an end to war would be a humanitarian blessing and a gold star for Roosevelt's presidency.

European powers were too biased to be suitable mediators. England was no friend of Russia and had a close friendship with Japan. France was aligned with Russia, and Germany was not unhappy to see the two sides continue fighting.

Neither side would trust the president if he appeared to favor one side over the other. Although Roosevelt privately favored Japan, his public stance was neutral.[86]

Sometimes diplomacy, like dressing one's person, is best not done in public. The president decided on a "behind closed doors" approach, starting with Japan. He cabled Griscom and gave him the go-ahead to leak quietly to the Japanese foreign office the president's willingness "to be of use" in mediating a peace settlement.[87]

Like his friend Harriman, the president had "started something."

Days passed with no response.

More days passed.

The president was tired of waiting. Hunting in Colorado would satisfy his need for action of some sort. Communication could be a problem in the high country of the Rocky Mountains outside of New Castle, Colorado—when it came to keeping in touch, Roosevelt might as well be on the moon. But Roosevelt's trusted secretary of war, William Howard Taft, could stand in for him back in Washington, and handle any crises that might occur while the president was off in the West.[88]

In April, the snows of winter still blanketed the cabin and tents of the Colorado hunting camp. Roosevelt and his companion hunted twelve-hour days in the cold mountain air. They used dogs to track and kill three bears on three separate days.[89] At night as he recuperated from a touch of malaria, Roosevelt read *Histoire du Second Empire*. In French.[90]

On April 26, the day after the president killed the third bear, Roosevelt's secretary, William Loeb, slogged through the snow to bring news. He had been manning the president's temporary communications center in Glenwood Springs when a coded telegram from Secretary Taft arrived. It was the text of a cable from the Japanese foreign minister, Jutaro Komura, that said in part, ". . . you will say that the Imperial Government, finding that the views of the President coincide with their own on the subject of direct negotiations, would be highly gratified if he has any views which he is willing or feels at liberty to give . . . in order to pave the way for the inauguration of such negotiations." In plain English, that seemed to mean yes, Japan would be willing to have the president arrange for direct negotiations between Japan and Russia.[91]

Roosevelt wired Taft that he would be back in Washington a week earlier than planned. Meanwhile, his absence from the White House had gone exactly as planned—it had enhanced his image of benign neutrality.[92]

The process was moving forward. Slowly. With one partner out on the dance floor, the question was: how could he persuade the other partner to dance? How could the tsar be convinced to take a seat at the peace table?

9

Albany: Uncertain Future

"A good organizer, a tireless and energetic worker, and a thorough master of the science of politics in all its different and complex phases and details . . ."[93] That's what one of the newspapers said about him. If even part of that were true, then why was he, Cal McKnight, still looking for a job?

As confidential secretary to New York's reform governor, Benjamin Odell, McKnight had jogged along comfortably for several years. When he wasn't snapping photographs of the governor on his travels, McKnight took dictation, typed a letter, fine-tuned a speech, handed out a press release, traded witticisms with a reporter, or exchanged pleasantries with a state senator waiting to see the governor. Variety was the name of the job.[94]

When Odell's term as governor ended in 1904, the former governor continued on as chairman of the New York State Republican Party. McKnight stayed with him, but the position wouldn't last. He needed a new job. When Odell decided to take his family to Europe, he made it very clear that, instead of the party's vice-chairman, Odell wanted McKnight in charge of the party's affairs while he was gone.[95] A New York paper reported on the unusual arrangement, and added that, "Mr. McKnight can keep quiet in nine languages."[96] He could now hope that there were employers out there looking for that particular skill.

Growing up as the youngest of four sons of a postmaster-storekeeper in Chambersburg, Pennsylvania, McKnight had first worked as a grocery clerk. When his family moved to Charles Town, West Virginia, he cruised timber in the Alleghany Mountains for the family lumber business. When his family migrated to Long Island, New York, he moved with them, learned shorthand and typing, and went on to work as secretary to a series of railroad executives. Eventually he served as cashier for the company run by Hudson Maxim, the inventor of smokeless gunpowder, who held the patent on a gunpowder that was fifty percent more powerful than dynamite.[97] Maxim was a brilliant inventor, but the companies he fostered rarely thrived. To an ambitious man, the future with Maxim Powder and Torpedo Company did not look promising.

The McKnight brothers looked after each other. The oldest, Stewart, was a lawyer who became a New York State assistant attorney general. That link connected Cal with the chairman of the New York State Republican Committee, Charles Hackett.[98] McKnight went to work for Hackett as his secretary, then for his successor, Benjamin Odell, who managed Theodore Roosevelt's successful campaign for governor of New York. [99] When Odell himself was elected governor on a reform ticket, McKnight went along to the governor's office.[100]

At thirty-seven, Cal McKnight had the world on a string. While he had no desire to run for public office, his strength behind the scenes was obvious, and newspapers reported that he might even be Odell's successor as party chairman. Life was good.

Fate, however, brought him up short. Instead of being exactly where he wanted to be, he was now a thirty-seven-year-old unemployed man with few job prospects and a wife and a three-year-old daughter to support. The only thing he had going for him was a small stenographic business, but that was not going to take care of them in the style to which they'd become accustomed. "I'll look out for you," Odell had promised.[101] But not much was happening.

McKnight's brothers wanted him to join them in a small real estate business on Long Island. McKnight, however, had developed a taste for the political life, and kept hoping, like Mr. Macawber, that something would turn up.

10

Washington: Dilemmas Resolved

Theodore Roosevelt had several dilemmas, and one of them concerned the Philippines. Congressmen from sugar beet producing states were complaining about competition from Philippine sugar.[102] The Filipinos, on the other hand, were pleading for relief from the high tariff placed on Philippine sugar imported to the U.S.[103]

He also knew that the Philippine independence movement was very much alive. During the Spanish-American War, Filipinos who had fought on the American side expected to gain independence at war's end. U.S. officials had other plans. Filipinos fought against American control for two years, but eventually the U.S. Army prevailed.[104] Some in congress, mostly Democrats, believed the U.S. should simply cut the Philippines loose to fend for themselves. But Roosevelt believed that the Filipinos would need many years of U.S. guidance before they were ready for independence.[105] A plan was already in the works to send a mission to the Philippines to listen to the islanders' concerns.[106]

The president was also beginning to worry about Japan. While publicly neutral during the war between Russia and Japan, the president secretly sided with Japan.[107] With its growing military might, Japan was now a major Pacific power, and the U.S., with its acquisition of the Philippines, had its own interests in East Asia.

If there were to be a peace conference, Roosevelt needed some understanding with the Japanese government about its territorial ambitions.[108] He was, however, not anxious for publicity's light to shine on the undertaking. Normal diplomatic channels would not do. He needed to send a personal representative.

Roosevelt's third concern was Alice. She was a journalist's delight, but a torment to her father and stepmother. Alice needed something to distract her from her pursuit of excitement.

A plan emerged. The president arranged to send a congressional delegation to the Philippines, including representatives from sugar beet producing states and members of congressional committees with an interest in the islands' governance. Under that cover, the mission could stop in Japan, where his chosen representative could discreetly determine what Japanese officials had in mind regarding Korea and the Philippines. He would send Alice along as his personal emissary to heads of state with the hope, particularly, of improving relations between the U.S. and China.

Happily for Roosevelt, his appointee to lead the delegation was someone whose personality and experience would be a good fit for the mission, and someone who could also keep an eye on Alice.

William Howard Taft and Theodore Roosevelt had been friends since Taft was the country's solicitor general during the McKinley administration. They had a common interest in "good government," and their friendship flourished. When Roosevelt sought an appointment as assistant secretary of the navy, Taft put in a good word and Roosevelt got the job.[109] Then in 1904, when Roosevelt began his first full presidential term, he asked Taft to be his secretary of war. Taft preferred the judicial side of government, but he obliged his friend and joined the president's cabinet.[110] Now, good friend that he was, Taft had agreed to lead this mission to the Far East.

Public service was Taft's expertise. He had a reputation for honesty, a reputation maintained through years of public service in appointed positions as prosecutor and judge.[111] At one time, he had been designated by President Arthur to be a district collector of revenue. After some time in the job, he looked closely at his situation and concluded that there were too many possibilities for corruption. He resigned.[112]

The son of a judge, Taft's dream had always been to sit on the U.S. Supreme Court. He had the assurance that comes from being a Yale man and a practicing lawyer with a strong competency in constitutional law. Later, as a federal appeals court judge, he had ample opportunity to study the variety of quirks in human nature.[113] When President McKinley offered him the opportunity to become governor general of the Philippines, his first reaction was to say no. His wife, Nellie, urged him to accept. He finally agreed, with the understanding that he would only remain in the Philippines for a limited time.[114]

Taft did well in the Philippines. Because he was close to six feet tall and weighed more than three hundred pounds, he cut a formidable figure, but the intricacies of social give-and-take came naturally to him. Those attributes joined with his genial, unflappable personality to enhance his popularity in the islands.[115]

But it was the measures he took to help guide the Filipinos to control their own destiny that earned him respect among the people of the Philippines. He used his knowledge of constitutional law to oversee the drafting of a constitution for the islands and set the people on a course which he expected would ultimately lead to their self-rule.[116]

Taft's service in the Philippines ended and he returned to the States. Theodore Roosevelt had become president, and Taft soon found himself on another detour from the road to the Supreme Court when he became the president's secretary of war.

Now Taft would be returning to the Philippines as the natural choice to lead the goodwill mission to the islands. He could tactfully shepherd the clutch of congressmen as they listened to the Filipino side of the sugar tariff issue. He could deliver the message to the Philippine citizenry that the U.S. understood their needs and intended their eventual independence.

Taft had experience dealing with other nations from working in Cuba and the Philippines, but he'd not dealt with the Japanese before. On the other hand, the task of discovering Japan's specific intentions toward its neighbors seemed simple enough.

And Alice . . . he would be super-chaperone to the president's daughter for almost two months, and he knew it might be the most demanding assignment of all.[117] He was fond of Alice, but even the Almighty himself would have to admit that her behavior could be challenging.

William Howard Taft, however, was not a shirker. He would do what he always did: he would do his duty as he saw it. Whatever would be would be.

PART III

PRELIMINARIES

June 1905

1

Tokyo: Turning Point

Russia's tsar intended to compensate for the losses inflicted by the Japanese on his fleet when the war began eighteen months earlier. Before the war, the Russians had two groups of ships in the Pacific: one in Vladivostok, the Russian port north of Japan; another in Port Arthur, Manchuria. It also had ships closer to home, in the Baltic. During the early days of the war, the Japanese had managed to put both of Russia's Pacific squadrons out of action.

Tsar Nicholas made a fateful decision when he ordered his Baltic Fleet to sail around Africa's Cape of Good Hope, across the Indian Ocean, through the Strait of Malacca, and past Singapore. The fleet was then to skirt around Vietnam and sail along the coast of China, pass Japan and eventually arrive at its intended destination: Vladivostok, Russia's Pacific port about five hundred miles west of Japan's northern island of Hokkaido. There, it could defend against a possible Japanese assault on the Russian mainland. Because of the tsar's decision, the Russian ships were where they were, when they were.

Admiral Rozhestvensky was put in command of the Baltic Fleet, newly renamed the Russian Second Pacific Squadron. No one had ever done what he was being asked to do: take a group of steam-powered, coal-fired warships halfway around the world without regular access to coal for fuel or dockyards for repair. He was expected to do this with crews of newly recruited seamen.

The voyage itself was heroic. It took them six months, including stops in Madagascar and Vietnam. Then, in the early morning hours of May 27, after a voyage of eighteen thousand miles (almost three-quarters of the distance around the world at the equator) Rozhestvensky's ships were soon approaching the Straits of Tsu Shima, off the northern coast of southwest Japan.

The Russian admiral's calculations had shown him that his ships did not have enough coal to take them on the safer Pacific route to the east of the Japanese home islands and thence to the northern straits to Vladivostok. The choice of the shorter Tsu Shima Strait was forced upon him. The fleet continued to proceed northward.

As they approached the constricted Tsu Shima Strait, darkness fell. The admiral ordered his ships to arrange themselves into a single line and to dim their lights. They began to move through the strait at a stately nine knots. Although Japanese vessels were checking the strait, the Russians miraculously passed undetected through the outer patrols.

Bringing up the rear of the Russian line was the hospital ship, *Orel*. International law required that hospital ships carry a multitude of lights so that they could be readily identified, and *Orel* was dutifully complying. As it happened, a Japanese auxiliary cruiser was returning from night patrol when her crew caught sight of the lighted ship. The perceptive Japanese captain identified it as a hospital ship and realized that the rest of the Russian squadron must be steaming ahead of it.

He sent word to his superiors. Admiral Togo and the Japanese fleet were on the far side of the island of Tsu Shima. They rounded the north end of the island and headed toward the tiny island of Okin Shima close to where the Russians had inflicted a painful defeat on the Japanese some months before. It was reported that Togo was anxious to cross paths with the Russians near the site of the first battle, with the hope that by intercepting the Russians amidst the spirits of the unburied Japanese dead, his men would be inspired to fire with enhanced spirit.

Whatever the motivation, when the battle began, the Japanese did fire with a vengeance—and with more powerful and efficient munitions than the Russians. They also had the advantage of ships that moved at fifteen knots, as opposed to the Russians' nine. The actual battle began in the late morning and the shelling continued until early evening. The Russian gunners had difficulty finding the range of the Japanese ships; although the Russians were firing, they inflicted little damage in comparison to what they received. The Russian crews wondered at the shells that hit them, exploding on contact and starting innumerable fires.

By the time the Japanese ceased shelling at 7:20 p.m., they had sunk four Russian battleships. Then, during the night's murky darkness, the Japanese sent in small, fast boats armed with torpedoes to inflict devastating damage to the remaining Russian ships. By morning, another Russian battleship was sunk, and three other ships had received mortal wounds and were eventually scuttled by their crews.

Two day later, after two more cruisers had been scuttled and still others had been sunk, the remnants of the Russian Second Pacific Squadron surrendered.

By the end of the battle, fourteen warships had sunk to the bottom (including some scuttled by the Russians), and the Japanese captured eight warships and sank three transports. They also took numerous prisoners, including the wounded commander of the Russian fleet, Admiral Rozhestvensky. The battle of Tsu Shima Strait was horrific, and it was the biggest naval battle the world had ever seen. In Japanese minds, the battle of Tsu Shima was a decisive victory.[118]

In Tokyo, the Griscoms had earlier seen the Japanese people's impassive response to military parades and were consequently astonished at the celebration that followed the news of the Japanese victory. In Hibiya Park across from the Imperial Hotel, bands played and dancers danced. Huge kites in the shapes of giant fish, lions, tigers, and monkeys flew everywhere. Colorful lanterns lit sampans in Tokyo Bay. Blazing tar barrels lit the faces of the thousands of people shouting, "Banzai! Banzai! Dai Nippon banzai!"

The battle of Tsu Shima Strait appeared to have tipped the balance, and a peace settlement was now a real possibility. Griscom had already informed Washington of Japanese ideas on terms. Two days later, the Japanese government made contact, informally and quietly, with Theodore Roosevelt.[119]

2

St. Petersburg: Diplomatic Skill

Back in Washington, President Roosevelt sent an urgent cable to his recently appointed minister to Russia, George von Lengerke Meyer. The minister's diplomatic skills were about to be tested. The president instructed Meyer to persuade the tsar to agree to send an emissary to talk with the Japanese about ending the war.[120] If Meyer didn't succeed, the war could continue, more men would die, and the costs would drain the treasuries of both countries. Roosevelt believed that Russia's government could be on the verge of collapse, and that Japan's government was financially unable to continue the war. He also believed that a peace conference was necessary before each side discovered the other's weaknesses. The assignment would require all of Meyer's wiles.

Tsar Nicholas and his family were at their summer palace at Tsarkoye Selo, outside St. Petersburg, when Roosevelt's cable arrived. Meyer had been the U.S. minister in St. Petersburg for only six weeks. He'd met Tsar Nicholas twice, but was no wiser about the tsar's position on the war than he was before. Now, sitting face to face with the tsar in the vast Alexander palace, Meyer stated firmly that it was necessary to end the war. If President Roosevelt were to issue an invitation, would the tsar send a Russian delegation to meet with the Japanese? Meyer emphasized that the meeting would not include anyone other than representatives of the two countries.

The tsar was not forthcoming. He was sure his people didn't want "peace at any price."

Meyer tried again. The tsar replied that he'd have to see what his people wanted. He seemed to have chosen to acknowledge neither the extent of Russian military and naval defeats, nor the revolutionary elements opposed to his regime.

Meyer was an experienced diplomat—he'd been ambassador to Italy for four years. He stood tall and straight and he had a direct gaze, a tightly controlled mustache, and poise to spare. He reiterated all of the president's arguments, the president's cable gripped tightly in his hand.

No response.

Meyer talked on . . . and on. He stressed the danger Russia faced. It had already lost most of its navy and stood to lose all of its Far Eastern territory if the war continued. Meyer swore that if the tsar agreed to the meeting, his acquiescence would be a closely held secret. There would be no intermediaries. Russian and Japanese representatives would meet face to face with no outsiders present.

The spring afternoon wore on. The scent of lilacs floated in the air. The tsar seemed unable to make a decision.

Finally, Meyer read Roosevelt's cable out loud, word for word. He emphasized the final sentence, in which the president said that if the tsar would allow Russian delegates to confer with the Japanese, Roosevelt himself would try to secure Japanese agreement to such a meeting, without mentioning that Russia had consented.[121]

Because Meyer had no knowledge of Roosevelt's communications with the Japanese, he was able to read this sentence with no sense of dissembling.

The president's cable went on to say that when both sides had agreed to meet, he would make a public request of each government and arrangements could be made as to time and place for the actual conference.

Still no commitment from the tsar.

Meyer talked desperately on, expounding on the president's character . . . the number of lives potentially to be saved . . . world opinion of the tsar . . .

At last, the tsar ended the meeting.

Back in St. Petersburg, Meyer cabled the president that, if the parties agreed, the tsar would send delegates to a peace conference arranged by the president only if his consent were kept completely secret.

For a diplomat, it had been a difficult but satisfactory afternoon's work. How it would play out, Meyer knew not.[122]

3

New York: Decision Made

E. H. Harriman was still thinking about Lloyd Griscom's invitation to visit him in Japan. He'd read news dispatches that said Russia and Japan were headed to negotiations that would end the war between them. A course of action was beginning to suggest itself.

Harriman had reached adulthood during an era when many Americans believed that the U.S. was destined to spread political and economic influence across the American continent. Now that its domain reached the coast of the Pacific Ocean, who was to say that U.S. interests could not be taken farther? Vast markets awaited on the far side of the Pacific.

Part of Harriman's mind was always at work on the next enterprise. Just as the century was turning, he had foreseen that economic activity on the West Coast of the U.S. was bound to increase, and that manufactured goods and raw materials would need to be transported from one side of the country to the other. Wall Street sources said that the 4,537-mile cross-continental Union Pacific Railroad was undervalued, and that—in spite of being in receivership—the line had been reasonably well-maintained and stood to benefit from an economy recovering from depression.

By 1905, Harriman controlled a continent-wide railroad empire. He had also gained control of the Southern Pacific Railroad and its subsidiary, the Pacific Mail Steamship Company.[123] Its ships called at ports in the continental United States as well as Japan, China, and the Philippines. Thus, Harriman currently controlled a transportation system that traversed half the globe. The thought of connecting the other half was tantalizing. That notion, mixed with his strong patriotism and belief that U.S. interests should have a larger share of business in the Far East, was beginning to suggest an audacious plan.[124]

The Russians had built railroads in Manchuria. One of them from Dalny, at Manchuria's southern tip, went north and was close to connecting with the trans-Siberian line that, when it was completed, would span thousands of miles from Moscow to Vladivostok. Japan looked likely to gain control of the Manchurian railway in the upcoming peace talks.[125] Jacob Schiff, Harriman's partner in numerous major railroad deals, had floated two loans to the Japanese government to help them finance the war with Russia. Railroads were Harriman's milieu, he had access to big money, and he knew how to get things done.[126] And thanks to his association with Schiff, Harriman had an entrée with the Japanese government.

A visit to the Far East and face-to-face discussions with Japanese officials would clarify the possibilities. He cabled Lloyd Griscom. Harriman and his family would arrive in Tokyo around the first of September.

4

New York: Travel Plans

At work, Harriman's passion was railroads. Away from work, his passion was family. As plans for a trip to Japan came into focus, Harriman realized that a visit to the Far East would be a unique experience for his wife, Mary; his daughters, Mary, Cordelia, and Carol; and his sons Averell and Roland. They would join him on this trip, he decided.

This would not be the first time the Harriman family would enjoy a grand adventure. He and Mary were able to enrich their children's lives in ways that few others could, and one of the ways they had chosen was travel. Six years earlier, Harriman had become fascinated by Alaska and determined that he and his family should see it. No ships traveled regularly to the parts of Alaska that Harriman wanted to visit, so he decided to charter a ship: the *George W. Elder*. The ship could carry up to 120 passengers, overkill for a family of six. After discarding the idea of using it for a fishing enterprise, Harriman's fertile mind conceived of using the extra space to carry along a scientific expedition.

In his usual way, without appointment or introduction, he presented himself at the office of C. Hart Merriam, chief of the U.S. Biological Survey. Harriman rarely made an effort to cut an impressive figure, and Merriam listened dubiously as the unprepossessing Harriman described what must have seemed like a grandiose scheme for taking a group of scientists on a voyage along the Alaska coast. Eventually though, Merriam learned the extent of Harriman's resources and his doubts turned to whole-hearted cooperation.

The 1899 expedition was a much-heralded success. The *George W. Elder* left Seattle at the end of May and returned two months later after sailing up the Inland Passage, along the Aleutians, and north as far as the Bering Strait. The scientists produced twelve volumes of data, still in use more than one hundred years later as reference.[127]

For a voyage to Japan, Harriman would not need to charter a ship. The Pacific Mail's Steamship Line included regular service to Yokohama. The scale of this trip would not match that of the Alaska enterprise, but E.H. Harriman never thought small. By the time the ship sailed from San Francisco, his traveling companions (in addition to his family) would include: their friends Robert Goelet and his wife; the family physician, Dr. Lyle; the children's tutor, Octavius Bates; two secretaries; two valets; and at least three maids. Also in the party was R.F. Schwerin, president of the Pacific Mail Steamship Company, with his valet and secretary.[128]

When he and Mary had the Griscoms to dinner months earlier, E. H. Harriman had "started something." Now his ideas had evolved, and he was about to see how he could transform them into reality.

5

New York: Shortage of Prospects

The four horses moved gracefully in their elaborate harnesses, trotting along together as if their moves had been choreographed. Perched on the seat of the short, stubby coach, the driver controlled these thousands of pounds of horseflesh with one hand, the reins of all four horses rigged together into one.

Twenty-three-year-old Mary Harriman, E. H. Harriman's oldest child, loved horses. Now, wearing a coachman's hat, with the lightest of whips in one hand and the reins in the other, she was driving her father's four-in-hand. It was the most challenging form of carriage driving, not a sport for the faint of heart. Tearing along with the horses under her control was bracing, joyous, and spirit-lifting. Few young women her age would have dared to try it.

Mary pulled up in front of the carriage house, stepped down out of the carriage, gave the reins to a groom, and headed toward the rambling house that was the Harriman home at Arden, where its seven-thousand-plus acres gave Mary plenty of scope for riding and fox hunting.

Four-in-hand driving wasn't Mary's only detour from the expectations for a well-brought-up young woman of her social standing. "Mary loved company," her brother Roland would say of her in later years. "She loved to dance and she loved great fun. She had a laugh that was most infectious."[129] But she had a serious side as well. Few girls at the turn of the twentieth century aspired to go to college, but Mary enrolled at Barnard and studied sociology. On field trips to Manhattan's Lower East Side, she saw thousands of immigrants crammed into tenements never meant to house such numbers. Those who lived there needed help with language skills and nutrition. Both children and adults required health care. Mary became a volunteer at the College Settlement House on Rivington Street and soon felt the need to do more.[130]

Mary was about to "come out," meaning she would be introduced to the social circle in which she would be expected to spend the rest of her adult life. A "debut," or official introduction to society, was like a wedding without a groom: the star of the evening wore a stunning white gown, and the party was huge, often in a hotel ballroom with flowers everywhere, a live orchestra, and favors for the guests. It was showy and expensive.

Mary pictured the young women she knew, dozens of young women like herself on the verge of "coming out." Instead of damsels in dreamy white dresses, Mary saw volunteers. She encouraged her friend Nathalie Henderson to join her, and they came up with a way to get the others involved. They recruited eight other debutantes to join them in writing "statements of purpose," promising that each debutante would become part of an organization to "contribute to the community."

Mary was only nineteen when she and eighty others went on to form the Junior League for the Promotion of Settlement Movements. They raised money for the settlement house, and twenty-three of them worked there teaching art, calisthenics, and music. (Eleanor Roosevelt also worked there, teaching dance to children and introducing her future husband, Franklin, to the plight of the profoundly poor.)

With Mary Harriman given the credit as founder, the Junior League movement spread across the country and involved well-to-do young women in supplying the needs of their communities.[131]

Mary was of marriageable age, but so far hadn't met any man with whom she wanted to spend the rest of her life. Dark-haired, strong-featured, and petite, young Mary was attractive and as lively as a well-brought-up young woman was allowed to be. The trouble was, as the daughter of E. H. Harriman, she moved in rarefied social circles. The young men in those circles didn't really seem to be interested in the things that interested her. Although it was exciting to consider going with her brothers and sisters on the upcoming journey to the Far East, the possibilities for expanding her social life were not encouraging. Someone once said, "The rich aren't like you and me," and that may be true when it comes to paying the bills—but when it comes to affairs of the heart, they aren't all that different. At the turn of the twentieth century, becoming an "old maid" could be as distasteful a thought to an heiress as to the scullery maid.

In the middle of August, Mary and her family would be starting for the Far East. Because her father put the same quality of energy into the lives of his wife and children as he did his business affairs, Mary was used to lots of family interaction. The trip would be fun. And in October, she'd be meeting her friend Alice Roosevelt in Tokyo. Still, for Mary, the problem of finding someone she wanted to marry remained. Bertie Goulet, the son of her parents' close friends, was certainly acceptable, and there was almost an assumption that he would be her choice.[132] So far, however, she had not leapt into his arms. What would time tell?

6

Seoul: Adventure's Promise

When he stepped off the boat in Kobe, Japan in the spring of 1904, Willard Straight was on his way to join the fraternity of frustrated war correspondents who'd been restricted to Tokyo while itching to get to the war's front lines in Manchuria. Being a war correspondent had never been Straight's goal, but the promise of adventure rarely failed to move him.[133]

Even as his feet hit the dock, memories of childhood adventures bubbled to the surface, triggered by the street smells of rank fish, the fragrance of pickled turnips, and the scent of bean cake. They reminded him of the colorful years of his childhood spent in Tokyo, and his first taste of the joys of freedom.[134]

Once, when his mother had sent him off alone in a rickshaw with a driver who'd been drinking, she warned him to be still and not aggravate the man. Instead, young Willard—who was all of ten years old—stood up and delivered a long harangue in Japanese (which he learned from the house servants). The driver was suitably intimidated and delivered Willard safely home.[135]

Now, as an adult, Straight was back in Tokyo—nowhere near the war, but scouring the city for war-related stories. He won no journalistic prizes, but he did enlarge his acquaintanceship vastly. He came to know the U.S. minister, Lloyd Griscom, Japanese officials including the elder statesmen, and the Japanese foreign minister, Jutaro Komura. Another of his acquaintances was Henry Denison, the American who worked for the Japanese Foreign Office, who provided insights into Japanese character and motives.[136]

When officials finally OK'd travel to the war zone, Straight was sent to Seoul and assigned to report political and general news of interest to the rest of the world. Such news was scarce and, if there were any, Korean and Japanese authorities usually wanted it suppressed.[137] With time to look about, his artist's eye focused on Seoul's streets. Although working people often wore plain, undyed white clothes, officials and bureaucrats could wear brilliant yellow, crimson, green, or purple, often in lively combinations. This made the street scenes more colorful and picturesque than those in Peking, Straight thought. The men clad in white garments stood out against the drab of the buildings, their fragile towering hats often cocked over one eye. Outsized umbrellas sheltered mourners as they walked along. Women draped their coats over their heads, leaving the sleeves to flap like a hound dog's ears.[138] Straight found the people likeable. When he wasn't scrambling to find reportable news, he sketched soldiers, sailors, housemaids, the men in the street, and his fellow reporters.

A short time later, Straight was sent to the battle sites in Manchuria to search out war stories. There he encountered Captain John Pershing, who was there to see what a military man could learn from following the paths of the Japanese and Russian armies and studying their fields of battle.[139]

Pershing, a West Point graduate, had fought in Cuba and in the Indian wars in the southwest U.S. In the Philippines, where Muslim Moro tribesmen were actively resisting the American occupation, Pershing was able to gain control by convincing them that the Americans were not there to separate them from their religion. A number of the chiefs became his friends. Only the few he couldn't win over did he subdue by military force.[140]

Wherever Pershing was, he grasped at any opportunity to travel. In

Manchuria, the ex-cavalryman and the artist-cum-reporter teamed up to see what was to be learned north of Mukden, where the Japanese army had finally dislodged the Russians. On horseback, Straight and Pershing trotted along the track of the retreating Russian army. Although the Japanese military had succeeded in defeating the Russians in northern Manchuria, the Russian army did not surrender. Straight and Pershing found hilly country lined with trenches used by the Russians to slow down their pursuers. The Japanese supply lines hadn't been able to keep up with the troops so far north, and the pursuit ended with the Russian army still largely intact, minus the troops lost in the battle for Mukden.[141]

The war stalled, and Pershing returned south to Port Arthur. There he made an extensive study of the Russian defensive trenches and the trenches of the besieging Japanese. To the casual observer, it looked as though the positions were impregnable.

"Up to that time there had never been an attack against a better-prepared defensive position, nor in modern war [an assault] more heroic and persistent than that of the Japanese," Pershing wrote of his observations.[142] By May 1905, there seemed to be little likelihood of further land battles, and Pershing's observational tasks dwindled.

Straight, meanwhile, had been busy profiling Japanese officers and men, including the head of the Japanese forces, Marshal Oyama. "One would never imagine that this simple, friendly old gentleman was the commander of 450,000 of his countrymen," he commented.[143]

Making his way south from Mukden, Straight sought lodging at Watts Hotel. There were no rooms available, but he was exhausted and needed a place to sleep. Looking around, he decided to bed down right there: on the hotel bar. He barely slept, thanks to a Greek, a Pole, a Russian, an American, and a man he thought must be a German/Russian spy sitting nearby, who quarreled over an increasingly violent game of poker. The game grew more and more acrimonious and the participants threatened to draw guns at any moment. The men continued to play until daylight, and their quarrels seriously interfered with Straight's sleep. Nevertheless, Straight called it "a great thing . . . my first taste of high life."[144]

While Straight was in Seoul, Edward Morgan passed through on his way to an appointment as U.S. consul in Dalny, Manchuria. He'd heard good things about Straight from a colleague at Cornell. When Morgan finally met the young diplomat, he was so impressed that he asked Straight to go with him to Dalny as his secretary. Straight, however, was still committed to his reporting job and had to decline.[145]

Soon after, Morgan was appointed U.S. minister to Korea and repeated his offer to Straight. Included in the offer was an appointment as vice-consul of the legation in Seoul. Straight knew that with hostilities winding down, his future as a war correspondent was limited. He accepted Morgan's offer.[146]

Straight left Japan in June 1905 to become a junior diplomat in Korea. His observant eye and agreeable personality would serve him well, and the people he'd meet would bring him closer to his dream of being involved in a large, meaningful enterprise.

7

Pine Knot: Rural Respite

The White House and its occupants were constantly the focus of the public eye. For the very proper Edith Kermit Roosevelt, raising a passel of lively children in the spotlight provided endless possibilities for stress. She'd found a simple retreat, perched in the wooded foothills of Virginia's Blue Ridge Mountains, where the family could occasionally escape perpetual scrutiny and relax.[147]

They had traveled four hours on the main line of the Southern Railroad, then driven ten miles by carriage—the president rode a horse—to Pine Knot, their unadorned clapboard refuge. Its rustic character, wooded site, and trilling birds suited the president, whose love of the outdoors was as much a part of him as his exuberant spirit.[148] "It is really a perfectly delightful place, the nicest place of the kind you can imagine," the president wrote to his son, Kermit.[149]

The remote location suited Roosevelt's purposes at that moment especially. The previous month had been difficult. When he'd received the telegram saying that the Japanese were open to having him facilitate negotiations, the president had cut short his Colorado hunting trip to hurry back to Washington. Persuading Tsar Nicholas II to send emissaries to a peace conference had been tricky.

George von Lengerke Meyer's cable said that Tsar Nicholas had agreed to send an emissary to a meeting to talk about terms to end the war if the Japanese agreed. From the White House, the president issued formal public invitations to both nations. On June 10, he was able to announce to the world that a peace conference had been arranged.

President Theodore Roosevelt's ability to bring the two powers together was widely praised, but the president appeared to avoid any close questioning about the details.[150]

Now at Pine Knot, he was able to sit back on the generous front porch and forget for a few hours the convoluted interactions of world diplomacy.

8

Washington: Rising Excitement

Feelings of love, hope, despair, and anxiety wrangled their way through Alice's consciousness. She had just returned from Cincinnati and a visit with Nick Longworth and his family. When she and Nick parted, she'd had the feeling that they were as good as engaged. But Nick had not had a chance to ask her father for her hand in marriage, and now they were going off to the Far East where there would be no opportunity for Nick to speak to him for four months. At the same time, Alice was enjoying the unfamiliar sensation of having her father's approval of her social prowess. He must have *some* belief in her to send her to represent the U.S. on a visit to the Chinese Empress Dowager Cixi, the absolute ruler of one-third of the earth's population.[151] Alice had acquitted herself well when she'd christened the Kaiser's yacht and when, at her stepmother's request, she'd helped entertain guests at White House receptions. She "met people well," and her wit had been sharpened in the best drawing rooms of Washington, New York, and Boston. But in China, she wouldn't know the language and would have to communicate through an interpreter. Spontaneity, often the soul of wit, would be difficult. How well would she do then?

Then her mind raced back to Nick. She did so want to escape perpetual parental judgement, and the only way to do that, it seemed, would be to marry.[152] But because Theodore Roosevelt was her father, her choices were limited: she could not choose a foreigner or a person of the opposite political party. Her parents expected her to marry someone of their social class.

Thirty-seven-year-old Nicholas Longworth was not every mother's notion of the ideal mate for her daughter. However, he did fulfill many of the requirements for the daughter of the president: he was an American; he was a Republican; he was wealthy.

The president was a Harvard man and a Porcellian—a member of an excruciatingly exclusive Harvard club. Being a fellow "Porc" made Nicholas Longworth automatically acceptable to Roosevelt as a suitor for Alice's hand. But Alice knew that her stepmother Edith took a dim view of him—she had warned Alice that Nick drank too much.[153] If and when Nick did approach her father, would her stepmother block the way?

Alice herself had certain specifications. Living, as she did, in the public eye and in circles inhabited by wealthy diplomats and politicians, she had discovered that her lifestyle required money. Her parents were not rich, and even in the White House, Edith struggled to stretch the family's income to cover the family's needs. And although Alice was fortunate enough to have her own income (from her mother's family), it was rarely enough to cover the expense of travel, dining out, and activities with her better-heeled friends. She decided she needed to marry a person of wealth.

Alice was her own woman and she had a sharp tongue, qualities that eliminated the weak and sensitive among her possible suitors. "Docile" was not in her resumé. Her parents did not dismiss the idea of an older man for Alice, perhaps feeling that someone her senior could restrain Alice's unconventional tendencies.

Thus, having found someone acceptable to her father and charming in himself, Alice was smitten. Longworth was experienced in the ways of the world, but never took himself too seriously. He was attracted to the vivacious, witty, and sometimes disconcerting Alice. And, of course, he could not have been unaware of the political advantage of marrying the president's daughter.[154]

Alice, however, was unsure of Nick. When he went away, she never believed in her heart that he would come back to her. For the next few months, they would be traveling together, well-chaperoned to be sure. She was thrilled to think that until October she would be spending part of each day with the man she loved. But would those months solidify the relationship, or would they end it?[155]

Warm weather had arrived, and Theodore, Edith, and the other children had left for Sagamore Hill earlier in the month. Alice found the White House unnaturally quiet. There was no tromping of small feet up and down the stairs, no calling of brother to brother, no one organizing a romp. Alice was left in a lonely state to gather her belongings together before her departure on July 8.[156]

She was pleased that Mabel Boardman would be going along. Mabel lived in Washington and was a good friend of the Tafts. She had been part of a group with a vision of an expanded, modernized American Red Cross, a group that had recently wrested control of the organization from the dedicated Clara Barton. Forty-five years old and never married, Mabel was a tall, strong, formidable figure, always up for fun. Alice adored her.[157]

Scheduled to go along as well were two friends closer to her own age: Mignon Critten from Staten Island, New York; and Amy McMillan. Amy's father, Senator James McMillan of Michigan, was charged with city planning for the District of Columbia. (McMillan's vision of an open vista from the Capitol to the Washington Monument eventually came to pass. He also designated the placement of monuments that still stand today.)

Thoughts about Nick, her responsibilities on the trip, and who was going along churned around her brain. They were almost too much, and Alice's body was complaining—in the past few weeks she had dropped five pounds and suffered the torments of indigestion, toothache, and eczema.[158]

Meanwhile, in her White House bedroom, Alice and her maid, Anna, looked about at the collection of trunks, hampers, baskets, and hatboxes that temporarily helped diminish the basic bleakness of her bedroom. Here, simplicity had given way to plainness: twelve-foot ceilings topped unadorned walls overlooking a wooden rocking chair and twin beds. The only decorative element was provided by the iron bedsteads, which were wrought in a severe rectangular pattern relieved by graceful finials on the corner posts and complex turnings on the legs. Nearby stood two heavy wooden wardrobes with mirrors on their doors, containing Alice's wearables. She opened the wardrobes, looked inside, and found herself face-to-face with the traveler's dilemma: what should she pack?

Because "Uncle Will" Taft and his wife, Helen, had spent several years in the Philippines, Alice had consulted them about the kind of clothes she'd need for the tropical climate and the events they would attend.[159] For formal occasions, she and Anna selected gowns that had seen duty when she'd been a bridesmaid for friends. They hauled out heavy linen skirts and dainty embroidered shirtwaists that would do for daytime. They laid out simple linen dusters and a small straight-brimmed straw hat to wear aboard ship. Then there were the enormous dressy hats with sweeping brims, dangling ribbons, jaunty feathers, and flirty flowers, and one with a life-size bird swooping from crown to brim. "And, of course," Alice recalled later, "there were riding habits and a special box for my side-saddle. I had things to ride astride in, too . . . underclothes were no small item, especially the petticoats with lace and embroidery, ruffles that even had small trains," Alice noted.[160]

Missing, however, was the customary women's undergarment of the time, which was a laced, boned, constricting corset designed to shape a woman's body into the silhouette of the day: high, prominent bosom, exaggerated derriere, and tiny, tiny waist. Alice disliked corsets, and her petite figure was slim enough that she could happily dispense with them.[161]

The carefully folded garments eventually filled three large trunks, one steamer trunk, assorted bags and baskets, and two huge hatboxes with hats arranged around the sides, crowns facing inward to keep them from being crushed.[162]

At last, there was time for Alice to re-read the letter from Nick that had arrived after her Cincinnati visit:

My darling girl: It is useless for me to try to tell you how I miss you. It really seems as though the light had gone out of the world. I am in the depths of despondency and if it was more than three weeks longer I don't know what I should do. As it is I can't pull myself together a bit. You were more charming than ever here. You were sweet to everybody and everybody was crazy about you. There wasn't a minute that we were together that I didn't wish it was an hour, and not an hour that I was away from you that I didn't wish it was a minute. It was a beautiful world when you were here . . .[163]

The excitement was beginning to build.

PART IV

UNDERWAY

July 1905

1

San Francisco: Westward Ho!

C-r-rack! C-r-rack! C-r-rack! Revolver shots rang out.

Alice Roosevelt was celebrating the Fourth of July.

As the train neared San Francisco, she had spent the early morning setting off firecrackers on the rear platform. Now she was topping off her celebration by firing her revolver at telegraph poles as they passed.[164]

Several days earlier in Washington, Alice, Taft, Colonel Edwards, Major Thompson, Mabel Boardman, and Amy McMillan, with their mountains of luggage, had boarded their private railway car, the Colonial, attached to the train that carried the congressmen, senators, and those wives who chose to come along.[165] One of the wives was Edith McAllister Newlands, accompanying her husband Francis Griffith Newlands, the U.S. Senator from Nevada. Edith Newlands was daughter of the dean of the San Francisco bar and, as Alice explained, "Mrs. Newlands was my own particular chaperone, and there never was a more charming, sympathetic and gay one."[166]

Alice had traveled extensively east of the Mississippi, but the western half of the country was all new and exciting to her, each successive vista like turning the page in an unfamiliar picture book. After they crossed the Mississippi, the plains seemed unending until, finally, massive mountains loomed on the horizon. The jagged peaks of the Front Range of the Rockies stabbed into the sky, appearing much closer than they actually were.

In time, the mountains surrounded them. The train moved through canyons and skirted the edge of rivers as it worked its way through the country's mightiest range and out onto the sagebrush desert of the Great Basin. The train chugged through the Sierra Nevada's green peaks and then dropped down into a less dramatic landscape as they approached San Francisco.

Alice threw herself into absorbing what she saw. "I had a little atlas that I used to read as though it were a romance," she recalled. As they passed through the West's dramatic elevations in summer, she marveled that she was in a part of the world where, come winter, trains could become trapped in the snow. Going through the mountains, she quoted to herself, "'We lead the iron stallions down to drink through the canyons to the waters of the West' . . . I was fairly jumping with excitement and interest."[167]

She spent so much time admiring the views with her friends that Uncle Will suggested she pay more attention to the wives of the senators and congressmen—invite them to a luncheon, perhaps?

Accompanying the Taft party was R.P. Schwerin, Vice President and General Manager of the Southern Pacific Railroad's Pacific Mail Steamship Company. The private car was one of his perks. About seventy feet long, a private car could include a full kitchen, dining room, as many as four staterooms, a secretary's room, servants' quarters, an observation room, and an observation platform. Light from clerestory windows in the arched fourteen-foot ceiling relieved the darkness of the mahogany paneling and the somber colors of the upholstered furniture.

Schwerin graciously offered the use of his private car to Alice, who soon invited the congressional wives to a luncheon in that rolling version of a penthouse suite. When the dishes were cleared and the ladies had left, Alice could feel that for that day, at least, she'd done her duty by the wives.[168]

When her father had asked her to accompany William Howard Taft's goodwill mission to Asia to be his personal representative, Alice had been delighted. Too, she was well acquainted with Taft, to whom she described herself as being "devoted." The revolver incident, however, may have triggered one of what Alice called Taft's "curtain lectures," as he fulfilled what he considered to be his responsibility for Alice's conduct. She later recalled that his lectures (always justified, she admitted) were delivered "more in sorrow than in anger."

"He was never out of temper," she recalled. "Possibly he was just a little too good-humored. I never had the least awe of him. I always felt that I could 'get away with' what it was he objected to."[169]

The real excitement for her was that Nick Longworth would join them in San Francisco. He and Taft were from the same district, and both were stalwarts of the Ohio Republican Party. Because Longworth was a member of the House Foreign Relations Committee, he had a legitimate interest in the tariff situation and U.S. governance in the Philippines.

The train finally pulled into San Francisco. Alice claimed she was so excited that she didn't sleep for the entire four days they spent soaking up the atmosphere of this frontier city by the sea. She was exhilarated by the air, the people, and the place that kept her on her toes all the time they were there. She was prepared to welcome any adventure that came her way.[170]

There were official engagements to meet San Franciscans: a luncheon at Bohemian Grove under a two-hundred-foot-high canopy of redwood trees; and another luncheon with the president of the university in Berkeley.

And then there was Chinatown, its colorful streets teeming with men clad in flowing garments, their hair in queues, speaking Cantonese dialects. Three-cornered pennants tagged its restaurants; beautiful, incomprehensible script lettered its signs. Its buildings housed gambling dens, brothels, and opium dens. Chinatown was forbidden fruit, out-of-bounds to a respectable woman—so of course Alice wanted to see it. Newspapers reported that she was seen there, but she denied it vehemently: "I did not go to Chinatown and treated with scorn all invitations to do so," she wrote to her father.

Her version of the incident years later, was slightly different: "I escaped my chaperones," she admitted. "I saw only the fringes."[171]

2

Pacific: At Sea

Amidst hubbub and confusion, *Manchuria* pulled away from the San Francisco pier. "Our bustling and shapeless departure . . . [was] very gay," commented passenger Elsie Parsons. "Perhaps I enjoyed most, as an anticipation of the East, the sight of our Chinese sailors and of the little group of Chinese women who waved goodbyes from the dock to their steerage friends aboard ship. To bring good luck, [those remaining ashore] filled the air with a shower of little colored papers."[172]

Later in the day, Elsie and her husband, New York's Representative Herbert Parsons, found themselves seated at Secretary Taft's table in the dining room. With his flock of senators and congressmen safely aboard, William Howard Taft could relax and prepare to enjoy an undemanding interlude as they traversed the vast Pacific.

One of his pleasures, obviously, was dining; he also enjoyed lingering at the table afterward for conversation. Taft presided at the head of their table, and Col. Clarence R. Edwards, bureau chief of insular affairs, anchored the other end. In between sat Edith and Francis Newlands, Mabel Boardman and Amy McMillan, Massachusetts Representative Frederic H. Gillet, the Parsons, and Taft's aide, Captain James K. Thompson. On Taft's right sat Alice Roosevelt, who had maneuvered to have Representative Nicholas Longworth of Ohio at their table as well.

It was a convivial group, reported Elsie Parsons: "Those of us who liked to hear him [Taft] talk—I, for one did, above everything else—moved down to his end. The Colonel and his girls (as we called Misses Boardman and McMillan), Alice Roosevelt, and Nick always left early. The secretary [Taft], Herbert, and I were very apt to outstay even the others." What they talked about "was not always of a serious character," Elsie added, "although Taft used to dub Senator Newlands and me 'the heavy middle layer.'"

Taft was impressed with both Herbert and Elsie Parsons, saying they added to the pleasure of the trip. In a letter to his wife, Taft described Elsie as "a bright woman . . . She was brought up in fashion but seems to break away from it some."[173]

In fact, thirty-one-year-old Elsie was teaching at Barnard College (the women's college affiliated with Columbia) and was writing a book titled *The Family*, which, had Taft known its contents, might well have unsettled him.

Like Mary Harriman and Alice Roosevelt, Elsie had difficulty fitting herself neatly into the expectations concerning what a woman should be or do. A rebel at heart, Elsie resented socially-expected customs—anything from shaking hands to saying, "Merry Christmas" or "goodbye." She simply refused to say the words. "Intellectually honest" was the way her friends described her.[174] She was a stalwart supporter of her husband Herbert's political involvement in the progressive wing of the Republican Party. With her master's degree in sociology, she had a sharp eye for what was going on in the world around her.[175]

Elsie's husband was one of Taft's allies in the effort to promote U.S. retention of the Philippines. Taft and the president believed that the Filipinos were not ready to govern themselves. A fair number of congressmen in the Taft party opposed the president on the independence issue. Like New York's Democratic Rep. Bourke Cockran, they did not see the U.S. as a colonial power. They would have preferred to see the Philippines cut loose, released from U.S. supervision and from the need for

U.S. military forces. One purpose of the Philippines junket was to bring these legislators over to the president's side by exposing the Filipinos' lack of readiness, as well as discovering the extent of the islands' resources and the marketing potential for American products.

It could have been a divisive topic, but it wasn't. Although Col. Edwards reportedly said, "We have all our enemies with us," the "enemies" got along amicably.[176]

Those on both sides of the issue would clamber in and out of dozens of small boats and endure an untold number of speeches in the effort to persuade them of the correctness of the president's position.

3
Washington: Obstacles to Peace

Back in the spring, before the Japanese and the Russians agreed to send delegates to a peace conference, Theodore Roosevelt complained, "Oh Lord! I have been going nearly mad in the effort to get Russia and Japan together." Now it was early July, and because the parties had agreed to talk to each other, he may have thought his troubles were behind him. But they were a long way from over.

With Taft and Alice—an odd couple to be sure—off on their missions to the Far East, the president could get down to the work of organizing the peace conference. In his invitation, he offered to arrange the date and find a suitable location. Because the Japanese had a long way to come, the conference could not take place until sometime in August. The Russians wanted to meet in Europe, possibly Paris, but the Japanese refused to meet anywhere in Europe—they suggested instead a Chinese city on the Gulf of Chihli, not far from Manchuria.

The meeting had to be on neutral ground, of course, and not in any of the nations whose neutrality was suspect. The president would not take part in the peace conference directly. His job was to bring the delegates from the two sides together and to find them a safe, comfortable, and secure site with access to reliable communications.

Each side had listed Washington D.C. as a second choice, but Washington in August was miserably warm and humid. Being hot and sweaty,

Roosevelt felt, would be unlikely to improve the negotiators' dispositions. But well-known resorts in cooler climes would be crowded.

Then the idea of Portsmouth, New Hampshire surfaced.

Portsmouth seemed to fit the necessary conditions: the little town offered cool sea breezes and several suitable hotels, and the navy yard offered a pleasant building for the negotiations themselves. Because it was a naval installation, access could be limited, and communications would not be a problem.[177]

Roosevelt was anxious about Japanese thinking concerning possible peace terms. Because of the decisive Japanese victory over the Russian navy in Tsu Shima Strait, and numerous victories over the Russian army, the Japanese believed that they had won. They believed that they were therefore entitled to a payment of money, or an indemnity, such as they had received after their war with China ten years earlier.[178] But Roosevelt had heard through diplomatic channels that the tsar had stated categorically that Russia would not pay such an indemnity.[179]

Sakhalin Island was another major obstacle to peace. The Russians currently possessed Sakhalin and feared a Japanese invasion. (Their concern was well-founded: by July 11, Japanese soldiers were in the process of occupying the island.)[180]

The president continued to impress upon the Russian diplomats that Russia could lose its own East Asia territories. Japan had won the war, and Russia needed to make peace for Russia's sake, he stressed. Paying an indemnity and surrendering Sakhalin would be a small price to pay to maintain Russia's presence on the Pacific. But much to the president's frustration, the Russians could not be moved on either point.[181]

At the same time, the president urged the Japanese to modify their position. He was fearful that if progress were blocked, the Russians would simply pack up and go home. The Russians faced an unstable political situation, and their continuance in the war could have easily led to the collapse of their entire government, a disaster for the Russian people.

From a world viewpoint, a government collapse would mean that there would be no one in authority to negotiate a peace settlement. The conflict between Russia and Japan could fester indefinitely.[182]

Finally, the arrangements were complete. The two sides would meet in Portsmouth, New Hampshire, in early August. With the meeting details in place, the president would have time for his usual vacation before the delegates arrived. Sagamore Hill, the family's summer home at Oyster Bay, Long Island, was an early version of a Summer White House. With the help of his secretary and the telephone, the president could conduct the nation's business from there.

In early July, Roosevelt and his family (minus Alice) escaped from Washington to Sagamore Hill's relaxed atmosphere. There, he ran the estate like a particularly fine summer camp for children. He had everyone up for games before breakfast, out into the forty acres of fields and woods for hikes and explorations or over to their private beach on Long Island Sound to frolic in its calm and salty waters. Whether the children were playing tennis or learning to shoot, Theodore Roosevelt was right in the middle of it, thoroughly enjoying his respite from the cares of state.[183]

Soon enough, the Russian and Japanese emissaries would arrive. The willingness of each side to change its position far enough to achieve a peace settlement . . . that was still the great unknown.

4
New York: Job Offer

Cal McKnight hoped the summons to E.H. Harriman's office meant that Harriman was going to offer him a job. Why else was he here? Governor Odell and Harriman were close neighbors and political allies, and Odell had indicated that he'd "look out for" McKnight—so perhaps that's what this was about.[184]

Harriman and McKnight were not total strangers—they knew each other from Harriman's visits to the governor's office when McKnight was Odell's confidential secretary. Harriman could be gracious, but it was no secret that he didn't spend time in idle chitchat.

Harriman greeted McKnight pleasantly, they exchanged remarks about New York's political situation, and Harriman got right to the point.

"How about coming to work for me?"

"As your confidential secretary?"

"That's right."

McKnight thought about the man he'd just passed seated at a desk in the outer office. He stammered, "But you already have a secretary. . . ."[185]

Just then, the phone rang. With a quick, "Excuse me," Harriman took the earpiece from its cradle and clutched the upright in his other hand. "Mary? Hello!"[186] His face lit up. There followed a lengthy one-sided conversation to which Harriman added very little.

While Harriman was on the phone, McKnight surveyed his surroundings. The office was all business: a simple dark desk pushed up against the wall; doubtless important papers filling its upright cubby-holes; a clock standing among a clutter of papers; and Harriman's coat and derby hat neatly placed over the very top.[187] The desk itself had five shallow drawers with carved handles, but the handle on the middle drawer was missing.[188] The handle-less drawer on Harriman's desk made this powerful man appear somehow more ordinary, more human. Otherwise, his reputation, his massive wealth, and above all, his manner, made him seem almost to belong to a different world—a world where handles didn't dare to go missing.

"It sounds like a good idea to me," Harriman finally said into the reciever. "Let's plan to go on Sunday." He ended the phone call and replaced the earpiece in its cradle. He swiveled in his leather chair toward McKnight and explained that he needed to go to see his son Roland at school and got right back to the subject at hand.[189]

"My secretary takes care of Union Pacific business, but he will be working under you. I'm looking for someone who's accustomed to meeting 'big' people and knows how to handle them. I'm leaving for Japan in the middle of August to talk to the Japanese government about a railroad I'm interested in, and I want you to go with me. Be gone about two months."[190]

Leave for Japan in less than a month? McKnight was knocked off balance, as if he'd accidentally tripped over a curb. "I . . . I . . . I need to talk this over with my wife," he stammered.

Harriman shot back, "We're sailing from San Francisco on August 16."

"That's just a few weeks away. I have a small secretarial business and I'd need to make some arrangements there," McKnight temporized.

"I need an answer today," Harriman insisted. "Tell you what . . . why don't you come as far as San Francisco with us? In the meantime, you talk to your wife, and see what arrangement you can make for your business.

We can talk in San Francisco, and if you don't like what you hear, you can turn around and come back to New York. And if you're agreeable, that's that."[191]

McKnight could see how Harriman had accomplished so much. When he knew what he wanted he simply rolled over anything that stood in his way. McKnight was left with questions. He hesitated. Harriman was known not only for his abrupt manner but for having small tolerance for the slow-witted and the slow-moving. Once he had a goal in mind, he moved toward it inexorably, refusing to admit that obstacles could not be overcome and insisting that those on his payroll utilize all their powers to work their way around, over, or through them.

Behind his glasses, Harriman's eyes were riveting. McKnight heard himself agreeing to travel to San Francisco.[192]

Harriman stood up. The interview was over.

Just as McKnight was opening the door to leave, Harriman said, "Oh, by the way, you can call me 'E.H.'—everybody who works for me does."[193]

5

Hawaii: Sugar and Surf

All they could see of SS *Manchuria* was its stern. Alice, Nick, the Newlands, and several others arrived at the pier just in time to see their ship leave without them.[194]

What would Alice's father have to say when he learned that his daughter, whom he had sent on a mission to heads of state, was not even responsible enough to be on time?

Alice and Nick had taken advantage of the ocean voyage from San Francisco to enjoy long hours together, sitting on deck or engaging in shipboard diversions. Occasionally sparks flew. Alice was uneasy and complained to Nick when he spent time with any other woman. He resented her complaints, tempers would rise, they would go without speaking to one another for hours or days, and finally, as lovers do, they'd make up.

All this took place under the watchful eyes of Mrs. Newland, Alice's official chaperone, and Taft, whose responsibility for Alice weighed heavily upon him. He got along well with Alice and wanted the best for her. "I quite like Alice," he wrote to his wife Nellie. "She is . . . straightforward and does not appear to be spoiled. In certain respects she is younger than her years. She is quite amenable to suggestion and I have seen nothing about the girl to indicate conceit or a swelled head."[195]

He was not so sure about the sincerity of Nick's feeling for Alice, however. In another letter to Nellie, he expressed his doubts about the couple's happiness should they marry. He complained that Alice spent so much time with Nick that she tended to neglect the other members of the party.[196]

Taft was also aware of Burr Macintosh, the expedition's official photographer, always alert for an unconventional shot. Because no engagement had been announced, Taft wanted no photographs taken that might show the couple closer than propriety dictated. When he saw the photographer approaching to take a picture of the couple, Taft's solution was to insert himself immediately into the picture. He either hovered next to them or placed his considerable bulk between them. But he couldn't be everywhere.

When SS *Manchuria* docked for a day in Honolulu, the party accepted an invitation to visit one of the large sugar plantations. On their way, local dignitaries inundated them with explanations of the sugar-growing process and finally, when they arrived under a canopy of green boughs and palm leaves, attractive young Japanese girls served light refreshments and beverages, strong and otherwise.

One of the non-congressional members of the Taft party was Lafayette Young, a newspaper editor from Des Moines, Iowa, who took the trip very seriously. During their brief time on Oahu, Young had focused on learning everything he could about the Hawaiian economic situation and on the details of growing, refining, and exporting sugar. When they arrived at the welcoming gathering that day, he was quite distracted from his mission by the pretty Japanese girls and the lilting Hawaiian music that floated throughout. In a dispatch to his Des Moines Paper, Young wrote: "A . . . band was present and stirred every man having warm blood in his veins with the native airs and the native dances."[197]

The lilting Hawaiian songs were so memorable that one of the members of the party purchased sheet music in order to try it out on the piano aboard ship. Young was disappointed. "They are far from being the real thing. The stringed instruments are lacking and the voices of the natives . . . cannot be reproduced by Americans," he commented.

Propriety dictated that Alice see the local dancers perform only a bowdlerized version of the hula. Not to be thwarted from the full experience, she later contrived to see an unexpurgated performance, and was soon doing her own interpretation. Soon enough, a new popular song in the U.S. proclaimed, "Alice Roosevelt, she came to Honolulu and she saw the Hula Hula Hula Hai, and I think before she reached the Filipinos, she could dance the Hula Hula Hula Hai."

"I could and did," was Alice's comment.[198]

Members of the party had a few hours free before the ship sailed, and they were drawn to the slender beach at Waikiki, anchored by the crinkled slopes of Diamond Head at the far end of its curving sands. Alice could luxuriate in the tepid, tropical surf, easily ten degrees warmer than the bracing waters of Long Island Sound where she'd frolicked with her father and siblings. She, Nick, and her friends were soon splashing in the waves and riding with the locals in their outrigger canoes.

Alice proclaimed it great fun, but that fun was responsible for their late arrival at the pier, to see that *Manchuria* had sailed without them.

But Fate smiled on them, and they quickly found a small boat and crew. "In a launch with Nick, Senator and Mrs. Newlands, and a few others, leis about our necks, regret in our hearts at leaving, I pursued the *Manchuria* out to sea," Alice remembered fondly.[199]

6

Tokyo: Fateful Conversation

Nick looked at Alice, his expression crushing, his voice as chill as an ice floe. "You know, I don't think I want to play with you tomorrow morning," he said.

A devastated Alice confided to her journal. "Oh my heart, my heart, I can't bear it," she wrote. "I don't know what's the matter with me. Nick . . . looked at me . . . as if he didn't like me, and said he wouldn't play with me tomorrow morning and I feel as if I might die. He will go off and do something with some horrible woman and it will kill me. It can't make any difference, I can forgive him anything, anytime, but it hurts like it hurts . . . Nick, love me, be kind to me—I am crying—I am crazy with grief. Oh, my blessed beloved one, my Nick."[200]

A child of the age of "keeping up appearances," Alice cried to her journal but pulled herself together in public. She and Nick once again patched things up and kept up the routine of shipboard life. She was playing two roles: the very public one as her father's representative, and the private one of trying to conduct a courtship. Once in Japan, the public role would have to take over. Aboard the ship, she and Nick could spend time together as they struggled with Spanish lessons, listened to Col. Edwards give informal talks on deck about the Philippines, watched a mock trial, and dressed for two parties: one garbed in sheets and pillowcases, and the other in fancy dress for a costume party.

Alice found her other congressional traveling companions congenial, although later she said, "I felt it to be my pleasurable duty to stir them up from time to time," which she did by lighting up her cigarettes in their presence. No other women in the party smoked—at least not where they could be seen.[201]

The crew of *Manchuria* rigged up a swimming tank on deck, and Alice took full advantage of it. One warm day, she was too impatient to go to her cabin and change into her bathing dress and its accompanying stockings. Wearing her long skirt, petticoat, shirtwaist, underthings, and hosiery, Alice jumped into the pool. Bourke Cockran, a member of the congressional delegation and an old family friend, was watching. "It looks so comfortable in the pool that I'm tempted to go in just as I am," he said.

"Come along!" Alice called, and after a bit more persuasion, he did—clad in suit, shirt, and tie. The press made much of the story, "a story that for once happened to be true," Alice said (although they incorrectly cited Nick as her swimming companion). But the fully-clothed Alice and the fully-clothed New York Congressman cooled off happily.

Ten days after they left Hawaii, the party watched the shores of Tokyo Bay open up before them. Even before they went ashore, the peak of Mt. Fuji in the distance signaled that they could be nowhere else but Japan. The ship anchored off Yokohama, and a tugboat pulled up alongside with a band aboard playing "Marching Through Georgia." The musicians had practiced a full repertoire of Sousa's and other American marches and were determined to play them . . . over . . . over . . . and over . . . until three o'clock in the morning.[202]

Yokohama greeted them with a welcome that was unprecedented, certainly for foreigners. Signal pennants streamed from masts on ships in the harbor, and ashore, the American flag hung from windows and fluttered from flagpoles. As a particular welcome to Alice, crowds lined up along the roads waving the stars and stripes, shouting, "Banzai! Banzai!" It was as if the Japanese had turned themselves inside out to show a side of their national character they'd kept tucked away from American view until then. They had come out to see Alice, and Alice was thrilled by their greeting.[203]

The Japanese newspapers heavily publicized Theodore Roosevelt's role in getting the two warring parties to agree to meet. The war had been grueling for the Japanese people, and the crowds had the sense that the American president would help them achieve the popular goals of a monetary payment from Russia and permanent acquisition of the island of Sakhalin.[204] They were honored that the president had sent his daughter to their country, and they honored Alice as her father's representative.

Lloyd Griscom, the U.S. minister, met the delegation in Yokohama. He personally escorted Alice to Tokyo aboard a train pulled by a locomotive decked in red, white, and blue bunting. Peasants working in the fields raised their arms in salute, and rousing cheers and *banzai*s continued along the way. Alice grabbed Griscom's arm and gushed, "Lloyd, I love it! I love it!"[205]

At the Tokyo station, a phalanx of top-hatted Japanese government officials and two young princesses clutching bouquets of flowers waited to greet them. The congressmen were slated to stay at the homes of various officials, while Secretary Taft and his staff would stay at the Shiba Palace.[206]

The Japanese invited Alice to stay at one of the royal palaces, but Griscom felt he had to discourage her from accepting. He observed that the Japanese seemed to regard Alice as an American princess, but to Griscom's way of thinking, the American public needed to know that Alice was still a real American girl and had not had her head turned by the adoring crowds or by associating with royalty. Americans had turned their backs on royalty one hundred and twenty-nine years earlier, and Griscom didn't want Alice turned into the symbol of a concept to which Americans were opposed.

"Why don't you just come and stay with Elsa and me?" he suggested, emphasizing that it would not be a good idea for the American public to believe that Alice thought she *was* a princess.[207] Alice pondered Griscom's argument. She had to agree. But she did like those *banzai*s!

Alice gracefully declined the Japanese invitation and went to the U.S. legation. Staying with the Griscoms (who were old friends) would give a better indication of her true status, and "no people were ever better hosts," she declared.[208]

The day after their arrival, Alice, Taft, the senators, and the congressmen jostled along in carriages as they made their way toward the emperor's residence. Ahead were the distinctive pendant lamps on the Nayubashi Bridge, spanning the moat in front of the imperial castle itself. The castle stretched high above the dark walls on the far side of the water, looking more like the residence of a well-to-do English squire than that of a Japanese potentate. The base of soot-dark stone supported stark white walls with simple rectangular windows. Topping the walls were roofs of somber deep gray tile, with corners that seemed to be reaching for the heavens. As they drew closer, they could see that the residence was not as plain as it appeared from a distance. Simplicity did indeed mark the lower stories, but sculptures of writhing feathered dragons capped the roof, and heavy bas relief adorned the pediments.

Inside the palace, His Imperial Majesty the Emperor of Japan, Mitsuhito, was prepared to receive them in a private audience. He was only fourteen years old when he was crowned emperor after the shoguns were deposed. Although Mitsuhito was his name, it was never used in official communications; rather, he was known as "the Meiji Emperor," and later as "Meiji the Great," and the "great enlightened one."

Herbert Parsons noted sartorial difficulties among the congressmen: "Most of us wore white gloves. McKinley of Illinois loaned his left to Otjen of Wisconsin and wore his right. As our turns came in close file we bowed at the sill of the room, advanced three or four steps and bowed again and then advanced, shook hands with his majesty and bowed, Griscom standing to the Son of Heaven's left and announcing our names. Driscoll's shoes squeaked horribly."[209]

The emperor provided a luncheon to his guests that was served Western-style, with one Japanese dignitary sitting between two Americans around the table. Even with the services of an interpreter and a plethora of politicians, lack of a common language meant that conversation flowed more like a desert trickle than a stream in flood.

The stiffness of the occasion was relieved as the meal ended and the emperor invited all fifty or so of his guests to see the private imperial garden.[210] Lloyd Griscom recalled later, "We climbed into imperial barouches and drove through a narrow gate in a high green fence surrounding a beautiful park. In front of us was a lake covered with pink flowering lotus. We walked across an old mossy stone bridge, sharply arched in the middle, and reached a forested island, crisscrossed by little trails." Then, a sound met their ears that few of the visitors had ever heard: the trills of a nightingale. The unexpected serenade added an exotic musical flourish to an unforgettable day.

Everyone was still delighting in the visit to the emperor's garden when Viscount Chinda, a member of the Japanese diplomatic corps, took Lloyd Griscom aside. He explained that neither he nor any of the other Japanese officials present had ever expected to view inside the emperor's private preserve. "We are very grateful to you," said Chinda, "for making this experience possible for us."[211]

The day after their reception by the emperor, royal gifts arrived for Alice, whose love of a gift (or "loot" as she called it) was legendary. "My family used to say it would have to be a nailed-down, red-hot stove for me not to carry it off," she said later. The empress (who, they'd been told, had been out of town the previous day) sent elegant gifts of embroidered gold cloth, an embroidered screen, a lacquer box, and a picture of herself.

The Griscoms took their job of entertaining their guests seriously, and together with Japanese officials, had planned a program to fill their few days in Japan before going on to the Philippines. Lloyd and Elsa had arranged an important event at the legation, one that Griscom termed "a monster garden party."[212] On the designated day, the American and Japanese women all appeared in white, tight-waisted, full-skirted glory. Alice dripped a waterfall of ruffles: ruffled sleeves, ruffled skirt cascading to the floor, ruffles cocooning even her parasol. The other women were similarly burdened, if not with ruffles, then with lace and tucks and ribbons and petticoats. All had chosen lofty, wide-brimmed hats, each topped with its owner's particular choice of streamers, bows, or flowers, and in some cases, graced with a final flourish of plumes.[213] As they made their way about the garden, they could have passed for a strolling 1905 edition of the fashion magazine, *Godey's Ladies' Book*.

As a guest of honor, Alice shared the distinction with two Japanese princesses, Nashimoto and Higashe-Fushimi. A special matting was placed for all three to stand on, and all the Japanese women who approached the princesses dropped into curtsies and then, to Alice's amazement, turned and curtsied to her. "The mere physical proximity to their venerated royalties caused me to become, for the time it lasted, an object of respect. It was real 'magic,'" Alice said.[214] She was not "real royalty," but she certainly did enjoy being treated as if she were.

Not quite so magical was an exhibition of sumo wrestling at one of the other garden parties to which they were invited. Remarking that the wrestlers were "as big as Secretary Taft himself," Alice thought that the Westerners "did not really appreciate the fine points of their slow, heaving performance."[215]

The Americans had been quite comfortable at the emperor's luncheon where the food was served Western-style—not so at the banquet given by the Mitsui banking family at the Maple Club, where the Japanese-style service was a formidable challenge for their guests. As they entered, they had to remove their shoes. Then, the men were directed to an upstairs dining room while the women went to a room on a lower level to be served separately.

They were to dine without benefit of chairs, which meant each man had to lower himself to the floor as best he could. Senators and congressmen, many of them middle-aged and of substantial proportions, all togged out in their dinner clothes, struggled and finally, finally arrived at the floor. Nick Longworth was the exception, quickly arranging himself, tailor-fashion, knees spread flat.

Not so Secretary Taft. He was an extremely large man, possibly weighing over three hundred pounds, and, while he was limber on the dance floor, his muscles were not in the habit of taking all that avoirdupois down to the floor. Like his fellow sufferers, he struggled. He attempted deep-knee bends, he twisted, he turned, he stooped, but he might as well have been trying to reach one of the other planets. The thought may have crossed his mind, "If I do manage to get down, how will I get up?" He may well have found himself distressed by the vision of the leader of this distinguished delegation stranded like a piece of flotsam on a shoal of Japanese matting. Mercifully, his hosts, seeing his difficulties, finally provided him a chair, from which he could survey the entire scene.

He looked down on the diners while the diners looked on with interest (and possibly dismay) as they were presented with quail complete with wings, head, and tail feathers. Each American picked at his quail and struggled with uncooperative chopsticks in an effort to move the rice from its bowl to his mouth. But at the end of the meal, hunger prevailed.

Later, the men and women reunited, and welcome sandwiches and champagne appeared. As everyone enjoyed food they could sink their teeth into, Alice turned to Lloyd Griscom. "Do you see that old, bald-headed man scratching his ear over there?" she leaned in to ask.

Griscom looked across the room. "Do you mean Nicholas Longworth?"

"Yes."

"Can you imagine any young girl marrying a fellow like that?"

"Why Alice, you couldn't find anyone nicer," replied the diplomat.

"I know. I know. But this is a question of marriage."

The exchange ended, and Griscom moved away.[216]

Social events aside, William Howard Taft had work to do. He needed to attend to the diplomatic aspect of his visit: his mission to extract information about Japanese territorial intentions. On the morning of July 27, a day or so before the Americans were to leave Tokyo, Taft and Prime Minister Katsura met in a simple room in Shiba Palace.[217] It was understood that although Taft had come halfway around the world to talk to the Japanese prime minister, Katsura was just as anxious to talk face to face with Taft, President Roosevelt's personal emissary. Their conversation was long and confidential. Only two other people were present: the interpreter and the Japanese foreign vice-minister.

Pro-Russian elements in the U.S. had suggested that a Japanese victory would inspire Japan to turn a covetous eye toward the Philippines, now a responsibility of the United States. Secretary Taft told the prime minister that it was his opinion that "Japan's only interest in the Philippines would be . . . to have these islands governed by a strong and friendly nation like the United States." The Japanese prime minister stated that he absolutely agreed with Taft's views, and asserted in the strongest terms that his country "harbored no aggressive designs whatever on the Philippines."

Count Katsura went on to say that "the maintenance of general peace in the extreme East forms the fundamental principle of Japan's policy. Such being the case, the best (and in fact the only) means for accomplishing the above object would be to form good understanding between the three governments of Japan, the United States, and Great Britain."

Taft was quick to explain that the U.S. had a long tradition of avoiding entangling alliances and that the U.S. Senate would have to ratify any international treaty. The likelihood of a senate majority voting to do that was in the neighborhood of zero, he emphasized. He thought that in practice, however, it was likely that the interests of the three nations would mean that they would stand together.

Katsura wanted to talk about Korea. He said he believed that Korea had been a direct cause of the war with Russia and he made Japan's position clear. "If left to herself after the war, Korea will certainly draw back to her habit of improvidently entering into agreements or treaties with other powers, thus resuscitating the same international complications as existed before the war. In view of the foregoing circumstances, Japan feels absolutely constrained to take some definite step with a view to precluding the possibility of Korea falling back into her former condition and of placing us again under the necessity of entering upon another foreign war."

Taft responded that "the establishment by Japanese troops of a suzerainty over Korea to the extent of requiring that Korea enter into no foreign treaties without the consent of Japan was the logical result of the present war and would directly contribute to permanent peace in the East." He believed that the president would agree with this assessment.

There was no treaty, no written agreement, merely a conversation. Each side expressed its views, the other side agreed, and that was that. The secretary worried, however, that he might have stretched the boundaries of his mission. He emphasized to the Japanese prime minister that the president himself would have to confirm what came to be known as the Taft-Katsura Memorandum, "a memorandum of understanding." Taft cabled Roosevelt immediately to make sure that the views he'd expressed were in accordance with the president's.

Because Roosevelt was relieved to hear that Japan had no hostile intentions toward U.S. Pacific possessions, and because he believed that Korea would be better off under Japanese control than as it had been under a weak and corrupt monarchy, he cabled back immediately. "Your conversation with Count Katsura," he assured Taft, "is absolutely correct in every respect. Wish you could state to Katsura that I confirm every word you have said."[218]

Thus was Korea's fate determined for the next forty years.

In the meantime, another member had been added to the party. Helen Frances Warren Pershing was a bride, married less than a year to John Pershing, military attaché to the U.S. legation in Tokyo. Her husband was almost twenty years her senior, but after she'd met him at a dance at Fort Myer, she wrote a friend, "I've lost my heart irretrievably to Captain Pershing." In and about Washington, their courtship was progressing at a leisurely pace until one day, early in January 1905, Secretary Taft sent for Pershing to tell him he wanted to send him to Japan as military attaché.

Pershing was put in the position of having to tell Taft something no one else knew.

"But, Mr. Secretary, I'm engaged to be married."

Taft congratulated him and asked the name of the young lady.

"Frances Warren," Pershing replied.

"You are a very lucky dog," Taft commented and added that Pershing wouldn't have to sail for Japan until February.

A whirl of wedding plans ensued. Because Frances' father was a U.S. senator, the elite of Washington—including President and Mrs. Roosevelt—graced the pews of Epiphany Church on January 26 for the grand event. The U.S. Senate recessed so that members could attend.

The day after the wedding, the newlyweds started for Japan. They honeymooned aboard SS *Korea* as it made its deliberate way across the Pacific. Also on board were General and Mrs. Arthur MacArthur. Both the general and Pershing were to be observers of the war between Russia and Japan.

In Tokyo, the Pershings settled into the Imperial Hotel. Pershing paid his respects to Lloyd Griscom and the Japanese secretary of war and, shortly thereafter, set off with General Macarthur for Manchuria and the fighting. Frances Pershing was left to find her own rung on the legation wives' social ladder.

Soon Frances learned that her father, who represented Wyoming in the U.S. Senate, would be coming with her mother to Japan as members of Secretary Taft's mission to the Philippines. She'd not expected to see her parents until John's tour of duty ended. Now she would not only be seeing them, but arrangements were made for her to join the Taft party and accompany them on to the Philippines.[219]

The Taft party had only been in Japan five days, but Secretary Taft had already accomplished his secret mission, and Alice and the delegation had paid their respects to the emperor. Taft gathered the party together for the next leg of the trip. Their departure from Tokyo became another exuberant public event with crowds blocking their way. As Taft and Alice made their way to Tokyo's Shimbasi Station, they were dazzled by the lights of thousands of lanterns. People in the crowds tossed bunches of flowers at Alice. As the train left the station, the air once again resounded with cries of "Banzai! Banzai!"

"Never had there been such a demonstration for foreigners," Lloyd Griscom commented.[220]

Alice appreciated that the Japanese had extended themselves for her and noted, "No people have ever been treated with greater consideration and kindliness than we were by the Japanese, not only Mr. Taft and myself, but the entire party."[221]

When, however, she and her friends returned to Tokyo weeks later, they would find the populace in an entirely different mood.

But now it was on to the Philippines.

PART V

IN BOATS LARGE AND SMALL

August 1905

1

Oyster Bay: Historic Introductions

For Theodore Roosevelt, sober contemplation led to the conclusion that the fate of nations might well rest on the two men he'd introduced this day. By four o'clock on the day the Russian and Japanese delegates met, the deed was done. President Roosevelt was back ashore at Sagamore Hill, looking weary but feeling that he'd done all he could to make the day go smoothly.[222] His goal had been to deal even-handedly with both delegations to avoid any appearance of favoritism, a stressful endeavor since his sympathies lay largely with the Japanese.[223]

The past weeks had been difficult. "The devil is in the details" certainly proved true for the peace talks. Both sides had felt obliged to argue minor points regarding the setting for their meeting. Negotiators had eventually smoothed out the wrinkles, and when the peace delegates finally reached the U.S. on August 5, the president brought them together for their first meeting aboard the presidential yacht, *Mayflower*, anchored in Long Island Sound.[224]

Jutaro Komura, the Japanese foreign minister, represented his country. His service in Korea, China, Russia, and the U.S. had provided him with a rich trove of diplomatic skills. Growing up, Komura expected to enter his family's sawmill business, but a relative stepped in and sent him to what later became Tokyo University. From there he attended

Harvard's law school, graduated, and returned to Japan, briefly serving as a judge until he went to work at the Japanese foreign office.

Komura was inscrutable—his face gave away nothing of what he was thinking.

He thrived on analyzing problems and was geared to the action that would soon follow. After his years in the diplomatic service, Komura and compromise knew each other well.[225]

Meanwhile, finding someone to represent Russia proved embarrassingly difficult for the tsar. After the job had been turned down by two ambassadors and several other prominent Russians, the tsar reluctantly appointed a man he detested: Count Sergei Witte. Not only had Witte opposed the war, he'd been active with a group of businessmen who'd sought to end it. Since he had done nothing to aid the war effort, Witte was a reasonable choice to negotiate its conclusion.

Because he had openly spoken against the war, Witte found it impossible to refuse.[226] From 1877 to 1897, he served as an official of private railway companies and was involved in the agreement that allowed Russia to build the Chinese Eastern Railway in Manchuria. The tsar appointed him director of the Department of Railway Affairs, and in 1892 he became Russia's minister of finance.[227] Witte had counseled against Russian expansion in Manchuria, but the tsar and his advisors ignored the advice.[228] The subsequent Russian expansion set off alarm bells in Tokyo, inspiring the attack by Japanese warships on Russia's Far East fleet. Thus, the war began.

The delegates had arrived in the U.S. and, on the day they were to meet, Roosevelt enlisted the U.S. Navy to transport them to the meeting site in Long Island Sound: Russians aboard USS *Chattanooga* and the Japanese aboard USS *Tacoma*. The boatswain's whistle's piercing note greeted both delegations as they were piped aboard the USS *Mayflower*, where introductions were to take place.[229] Once both delegates arrived, Roosevelt introduced the two men upon whom the fate of much of the world rested.

Although they were dressed alike in diplomats' togs—cutaway coats, bowties, and top hats—the two leaders were about as similar as a house cat and a lion. Komura was short and slight of build, with a pale complexion and an anxious expression.[230] Witte, on the other hand, was a burly six feet and six inches with an outgoing personality. He looked as though he could crush Komura with one bear hug.[231]

Both delegates were termed "plenipotentiaries," meaning that each theoretically had full powers to act.[232] Witte's deputy was the same Baron Roman Rosen who'd been given his walking papers from Japan eighteen months before, and who was now the Russian ambassador in Washington.

At the buffet luncheon, most everyone ate standing up, thus finessing the problem of seating guests according to diplomatic protocol. Only the president, Witte, and Komura were exempted, and sat together. As the meal ended, Roosevelt proposed a toast: "It is my earnest hope and prayer," he said, his glass held high, "in the interest not only of these two great powers, but of all civilized mankind, that a just and lasting peace may be speedily concluded between them."[233]

Roosevelt knew well what the obstacles were to an understanding between the two nations. He also knew that if the peace conference failed, history would be ruthless in its judgment of him.

2
Manila: Public Appearances

After Alice missed the boat in Hawaii, spent too much time with her love interest, smoked in public, and jumped into a swimming pool fully clothed, William Howard Taft could reasonably be expected to harbor some anxiety about what his charge might do next. But Alice's conduct in Japan had been above reproach. Once on foreign soil, she seemed to realize the need to don her more serious persona. A Japanese newspaper remarked upon Alice's "intelligence and resolute character,"[234] and Taft wrote to his wife that Alice was "prompt, gracious and courteous."[235] Perhaps the *banzai*s made her feel conspicuous enough that she could forego the unconventional and stop trying to raise eyebrows. Whatever the case, Taft was pleased with her behavior so far.[236]

And now, during the mission to the Philippines, Alice Roosevelt was about to show her grit and grace. Wanting desperately to justify her father's confidence in her, she'd made a good start in Japan. During their month-long stay in the Philippines, however, she'd need to soar above discomforts that could dishearten a lesser soul.

When their ship steamed into Manila's generous harbor, the passengers were enveloped in the steamy fragrance of the tropics. As the ship proceeded to its berth on the Passaig River, they could see the clutter on the docks, the motley variety of vessels bustling about the harbor, palm trees casting feathery shadows on the cobblestone, men strolling the streets clad in white against the heat, and all about, the looming spires, turrets, and domes of Manila's ubiquitous churches.

The architecture's Spanish flavor was surprising: the two-and-three-story buildings were pale, galleried, and faced with arcades, strikingly different from the foursquare, low, dark structures they'd seen in Tokyo. Instead of jinrickshaws, diminutive horse-drawn carriages transported Alice, Taft, and the other members of the party through the streets. They were on their way to the former seat of Spanish colonial government, the *ayuntamiento*.[237] The formidable structure was tucked inside the *Intramuros*, the walled city dating from Manila's early days. The Americans entered through elaborately carved doors behind five graceful arches that adorned the cream-colored façade. Inside, at the top of the double staircase, they entered a grand hall, startling in its dazzling whiteness—even the marble floor was white. On the ceiling, deep coffers framed colorful murals, and colorful flags flew from a balcony supported by classic columns topped with gilded capitals. Pictures of Presidents McKinley and Roosevelt hung behind the dais where the officials sat, and on wooden medallions nearby were portraits of the young Spanish king and the queen mother. Glittering chandeliers illumined the Filipino and American officials who welcomed them. What, Mabel Boardman wondered, might be wrought by this combination of indigenous, Spanish, Christian, and now, North American people?[238]

After everyone who needed to make a speech had made one, the Americans were whisked off to the homes of various officials, where they were to stay. Governor Wright had invited Alice and Taft to stay with him at Malancañon. With its white walls and red roof, Malancanon clung to the very edge of the Passaig River and had been the summer home of Spanish colonial governors. Beige Philippine marble paved the entrance hall, and on the balcony at the top of the grand staircase hung portraits of explorers Hernando Cortez, Ferdinand Magellan, and Cristobal Colon. The rooms on the lower level were public space and reasonably imposing. The family quarters on the second level were somewhat cramped and inconvenient, a situation that may have influenced Alice's reaction: "After all my youthful wishes to live at Malancanon, I found it a little disappointing," she confided in her memoirs years later. "It did not have for me the charm of the Spanish-American houses—the huge, somber palace in Havana and the Fortaleza in San Juan, though I liked my big, cool, dim-lit room where lizards of all sizes and shapes rustled about the walls and ceiling . . ."[239]

If she were feeling let-down about the palace, she was compensated by meeting Ann and Marjorie Ide, daughters of Vice-Governor Wright. The Ide girls, whose father was a member of the U.S. Foreign Service, had spent their early years in Samoa, at the same time that author Robert Louis Stevenson lived there. Stevenson learned that Ann Ide had been born on Christmas Day, and he felt that the Christmas child often comes up short in the matter of birthday gifts. Shortly thereafter, Ann's father received a formal letter with an enclosure which read:

> *I do hereby transfer to the said A. H. Ide All and Whole of my rights and privileges in the 13th of November, formerly my birthday, now hereby and henceforth, the birthday of said A.H. Ide, to have, hold, exercise and enjoy in the customary manner.*
>
> *Signed,*
> *Robert Louis Stevenson*[240]

Alice found the Ide girls pale and delicate but extraordinarily beautiful—and she was not the only one charmed by them. Bourke Cockran, U.S. Congressman from New York (the same Bourke Cockran who had jumped fully clothed into the swimming pool with Alice) had been a widower for ten years. With an Irish lilt to his speech, a gift for the flowery phrase, strong opinions, and a booming voice, he was a natural orator and a standout in any crowd. Alice found him enormously charming and amusing.[241]

Bourke Cockran was introduced to Ann Ide in Manila that August. His masterful way with words undoubtedly made an impression on Ann, and she made such an impression on Cockran that he couldn't forget her. When he left the Philippines a few weeks later, he took with him a memory of Ann Ide that would have consequences for both of them.

❧

The Filipinos well remembered William Howard Taft. In July 1901, President McKinley put him in charge of a commission to establish a civil government for the islands.[242] Later he became civil governor, replacing General Arthur MacArthur, military governor since May 1900.[243]

By the late 1890s, the Spanish had been in power in the Philippines for more than three hundred years. Five years before Taft arrived, a group of Filipinos rebelled. Two years later, as the rebellion raged on, the U.S. was at war with Spain and consequently supplied the Filipinos with arms. When Spain was finally defeated, the revolutionaries believed that they had achieved independence. Not so. The U.S.—believing that it had helped liberate the islands from Spain—did not choose to set them free. The U.S. actually bought the islands from Spain, reportedly for twenty million dollars. The Filipinos continued to fight, only this time they were fighting the U.S. Army in a guerilla war. There were thousands of casualties among the Filipinos and reports of gross misbehavior by American troops. The Filipinos declared the islands a republic at least twice before U.S. troops subdued them.[244]

General MacArthur still conducted military operations on some of the islands, while Taft's job was to establish a civil government. Taft did not believe the islanders were ready for independence, but he believed it was his job to prepare them to one day govern themselves. MacArthur's military action against the populace may have made Taft's job more difficult. Authority was divided.

The two continued to tangle until finally, a year later, Taft was appointed governor-general. MacArthur was relieved of the Philippine command, promoted to lieutenant-general, and put in charge of the Department of the Pacific. By 1905, he was military attaché to the U.S. legation in Tokyo, from whence he traveled to Manchuria to study the battles between the Japanese and Russian armies.[245]

After Taft arrived in the Philippines, his paternalistic approach included measures aimed to guide Filipinos to control their own destiny. He set up the framework for civil control. His background in constitutional law helped him as he oversaw the drafting of a Philippine constitution with a bill of rights and a court system. He imported U.S. lawyers to become judges and to introduce a form of justice that would apply to all, of high or low estate. He worked to establish a representative assembly and helped to build a merit-based civil service. Because of rampant illiteracy, he made education a priority and imported Spanish-speaking teachers from the U.S.

Due to the Catholic Church's vast ownership of land in the archipelago, Taft personally visited the Vatican to begin negotiations for the purchase of land that would in time be distributed among 50,000 Filipinos.[246] Forty years would pass before the Philippines gained full independence, but Taft helped put the basic building blocks in place.[247]

When Taft returned to Washington in 1904, he left behind new roads, better sanitary conditions, land reform, and schools. He was not beloved by those Filipinos who were still pressing for independence, but otherwise, he was the object of much good feeling and found hospitality unstinted on his return.

Once in Manila, instead of flouting convention as she often tried to do at home, Alice extended herself to fit in. In consideration of those who hosted events and those who came out to see her, she was prompt. She endeared herself to the Filipinos by wearing the local costume: the frothy, feminine *mestiza*, a dress made for her by Filipino women who reportedly labored for three months to create its puffy, billowing sleeves, draped bodice, and layered full skirt.[248]

August was perhaps not the optimum time for a group from a temperate climate to visit Manila, a city that lies less than fifteen degrees north of the equator. The hot, sultry atmosphere was a daunting challenge to those in the public eye. A man was expected to dress in a suit with a stiff collar and necktie, and a woman had to wear a skirt to the floor, a petticoat, an elaborate shirtwaist, and a hat the size of a serving platter.

At one reception, the tropical heat pressed down as they stood to shake hands with the hundreds of guests who wanted to meet them. Alice and Taft might as well have been encased in a damp sponge. At one point, Alice glanced at Taft, whose white linen suit had long since wilted, and saw that the rotund secretary was literally dripping perspiration. "I don't see how Mr. Taft stood it," she recalled. The round of events that Taft and Alice were obliged to attend was never-ending. "We were up and doing even in the noon heat when all sensible residents of the tropics were taking their noon siestas," Alice commented.[249]

On the Monday after they arrived, Alice and Taft showed their mettle again, dripping in the tropical heat for two hours as they took in an exuberant parade. To honor the president's daughter and the secretary of war, U.S. soldiers, local policemen, thousands of schoolchildren, and floats passed happily in review. Then there were the bands, bands, and more bands, before and after each unit (so their music didn't interfere with one another's). Then after the floats dropped out, the bands followed each other directly . . . each cheerfully playing a different tune.

For the parade's grand finale, firefighters led the way. A mellow Filipino pony sedately pulled a small water cart accompanied by a dozen men, on foot, each carrying a pail. Then, swooping down from the bridge farther up the street came the mighty modern American fire engines, as if to push the Filipino firefighters out of the way.[250]

Another day, Alice, Mabel Boardman, and Secretary Taft visited an all-girls manual training school and a normal school (for men and women) where English was spoken. Secretary Taft talked to the young people and stressed their future responsibilities. On August 30, Taft presided over a meeting that established the Philippine Red Cross as an insular chapter of the American Red Cross. Mabel Boardman—a board member of the A.R.C.—was named advisor to this new chapter. The branch remained a subsidiary of the A.R.C. until Philippine independence was achieved more than forty years later.[251]

The public appearances of Alice Roosevelt, William Howard Taft, Mabel Boardman, and the congressmen and their wives were designed to demonstrate that the U.S. was concerned for the welfare of the Philippines and Filipinos.

On some of the party, the mission took a physical toll. All of this activity required frequent changes of clothing. Alice's maid, Anna, was responsible for keeping Alice's wardrobe in event-ready condition, a formidable task when she had to wash everything by hand and heat irons on whatever sort of stove was available. At one point during the Philippine visit, Anna's health failed her, and she was sent to the ship temporarily to recuperate. Secretary Taft's valet was pressed into service, and we are left to wonder how he coped with Alice's ruffles and flounces.[252]

Mabel, like Alice, loved to dance, and while aboard the *Manchuria* they'd both learned to dance the *rigadon*, a French dance brought to the Philippines by the Spanish. Their instructor was Taft himself, aided by some young Philippine passengers. Somehow the dance, structured as a minuet, had been adopted by the Filipinos as an informal national emblem. At Saturday night's ball, held at the *ayunamiento*, waltzes and two-steps dominated. But when the orchestra struck up a *rigadon*, Taft and his students were on their feet and out on the floor. They bowed, they curtseyed, they promenaded, and they did a restrained version of the grand right-and-left, all part of the *rigadon*. Claimed Mabel Boardman, "We could dance it without being reduced to the helpless confusion that generally ends our own 'lancers.'"[253]

The next day they left Manila to embark on a two-week tour of the islands. Manila, however, would see them again.

3

Islands: Luzon to Jolo

Secretary Taft was leading a junket remarkable for both the number of participants and its geographic range. When he learned of the junket, Lloyd Griscom found the number of congressmen coming halfway around the world to investigate this island territory "astonishing."[254] Yet, here they were, about to venture to islands scarcely known to Americans outside the military. They were perhaps reassured by the steady hand of Taft, who at least had some knowledge of the area into which they were plunging.

"Army transport" had a grim ring to it, suggesting olive-drab paint and minimum comfort. When the travelers finally boarded USAT *Logan*, however, the ship proved to be a pleasant, comfortable surprise. Built as a passenger liner, it was purchased by the fledgling U.S. Army Transport Service during the Spanish-American War. The rechristened ship never took part in the war, but instead spent its army life ferrying troops between San Francisco and Manila. With accommodations for eighty officers and one thousand troops, *Logan* could easily take in the entire Taft party with room to spare. Its refrigerator could hold one thousand pounds of meat, all while the ship traveled at up to thirteen knots.[255] On *Logan*'s downside was its deep draft, which meant that its passengers spent many hours scrambling in and out of the ship's small boats to visit the islands on their schedule.

Still, *Logan* kept them safe and comfortable while they island-hopped to do what they had come to do: meet and listen to the Filipino people. Filipinos sought a reduction on the U.S. tariff on sugar, and they were anxious for the visiting legislators to understand why that was important to them.

The sugar-growing island of Panay was the party's first stop. The travelers—for the first of many times—clambered into small, open boats for the run up the river to the town hall, where, despite the morning hour, a group of local women wearing mestizo dresses and diamonds waited to welcome them.

Miss Lacson, a young woman of the island, accompanied the Americans on their morning tour. She had strong feelings about the tariff and implored the congressmen: "Please take off the sugar Dingley tariff, then I can have a little money to go to Washington to thank the senators and representatives for helping us here."[256]

At the banquets, the speeches followed a distinct pattern. The local speaker pleaded for tariff relief so they could sell their sugar at a profit. Others urged that the Filipinos be granted immediate independence. Taft was sympathetic to their tariff position, but on the question of Philippine independence he answered by saying, "I did not come to give you your independence but to study your welfare." On later occasions he was more direct: "You will have your independence but not until you are ready for it, which will not be in this generation—no, nor in the next, nor for perhaps a hundred years or more."[257]

When Taft had been governor-general, he'd become well-thought-of for saying, "The Philippines for Filipinos." But he did not mean what much of the population thought he meant. He meant that he planned to educate the Filipinos and oversee the writing of a constitution that would be the foundation for *eventual* self-governance, not preparation for immediate freedom from U.S. oversight. Taft's thinking was that, to govern themselves, the people needed more education and a stronger foundation, otherwise the government could fall into the hands of a few oligarchs. When Filipinos heard of Taft's return to the islands, some believed that he had come to announce the Philippines' immediate independence. Taft's stern words were intended to disabuse them of that idea.

Everywhere they went, on each of the islands they visited, Taft's entourage was treated to an overwhelming number of banquets and speeches—a treat that turned into boredom for some, torture for others. The banquets featured Western-style food and unfamiliar fruit—mangos, lanzones, and chicos—popular with the Philippine ladies. Speeches by local leaders expressed discontent with the sugar market situation and, of course, with the high U.S. tariff.[258]

Alice was always seated at the head table just in front of the interpreter and noted, "The local head official would speak in Spanish, Mr. Ferguson, the interpreter, would bellow it paragraph by paragraph in English, Mr. Taft would reply in English, and the interpreter would repeat his performance, this time in Spanish . . . my eardrums ached.[259]

Lafayette Young was another who took a dim view, expressed in an article in the Des Moines Capital newspaper: "The party is growing weary of banquets, a series of interruptions that began in Japan. The banquets have done more to wear out the party than all their labors, and in most respects they have been a positive hindrance to the real purpose of the expedition."[260]

Toward the end of the tour, some in the party avoided these events, but Alice did not have that luxury. She was expected to appear, and appear she did. But she managed to find a diversion from the speeches: ants.

By speech time, the food on the table would be in a semi-liquid state and the first ant would crawl into view. Alice would arrange bits of the food into a trail of what she called "moist temptations." The trail would lead the ants to the main event and the inevitable result was ants everywhere. Taft, seated only a few feet away, looked on with dismay.

The ants evoked one of Taft's remonstrations. He told Alice that he did not want the feelings of their hosts to be hurt. Neither did Alice, so that diversion stopped.[261]

They soon approached the island of Negros, an island where an apparently inactive eight-thousand-foot-high volcano brooded over the fertile coastal lowlands. As in many places, *Logan* could not make a close approach. Those who wanted to go ashore would have to get there in the ship's small boats. The sea's heavy chop discouraged several of the women, but Mabel Boardman, always ready for any activity, and Alice, child of her intrepid father, were among the few to make the rough passage.

When they reached calmer water near shore, local craft conveyed them to an enormous bamboo raft that awaited them. Rumor had it that their hosts had constructed the raft especially for the occasion, and a magnificent creation it was: perhaps fifty feet long; hung about with curtains, lanterns, and flags; girded by an elaborately braided railing; and draped with looping garlands of rope.

While the men listened to more laments about the state of the sugar industry, the governor's wife whisked the women off for a drive in her carriage and then to her home, where they tried their best to chat with a cadre of local women, few of whom spoke English.

A ten-year-old girl performed on the piano and a young woman greeted them in Spanish, calling them "the fair flowers of America." Later, in the governor's carriage once more on their way to yet another banquet, the driver and the ponies had a difference of opinion about where they were supposed to go. The ponies won, and the women were treated to several extra turns around the plaza before the ponies decided to stop at the banquet site, a pavilion in the center of the plaza.

The travelers recalled their complex morning voyage from the ship, knowing they would have to repeat it in reverse. After the women rejoined the men, they all put in a brief appearance at the banquet. When they opted to leave early, however, they left behind disappointed local orators whose carefully prepared speeches now lacked an audience.[262]

Aboard *Logan* once more, the Americans headed to the port of Zamboanga, on the southwest end of the island of Mindanao. There, the colors of Zamboanga's harbor dazzled: turquoise water, lush green mountains, and overhead, blue sky dappled with whipped cream clouds. *Vintas,* the small Moro outrigger vessels, flashed by, their square sails vertically striped in brilliant reds, yellows, and greens.

Ashore, the travelers shopped for native handwork including large machete-like knives called bolos. Mabel Boardman overheard a Moro man explaining to one of the Americans what he should consider before he purchased one: "You need to buy bolo with a rough handle," he advised, "because when it drips with blood, a silver handle you cannot grip." Although several Americans invested in bolos, there is no record of how many felt the need for a rough handle.[263]

The travelers were leaving Mindanao. They would return, but first they were expected at Jolo in the Sulu Archipelago, a chain of islands that dangles at the southwest end of the Philippines. Jolo was the farthest extent of the mission, and their visit turned out to be the kind of memory one dredges up on dark, dismal days when there is a need to recall a time of sun and joy.

Jolo's police force welcomed them: they stood in two straight rows, one on either side of the walkway, facing each other, in trim khaki uniforms. Because they were Muslims, each one wore a fez. Each one stood at attention and each was as barefoot as the day he was born.[264] Alice, Taft, and the other Americans proceeded to the parade ground that anchored the military post. There, the island's prominent chieftains, or dattos, were assembled with their parasol-bearers and betel-nut carriers. Thousands of tribesmen had journeyed from neighboring islands to add to the Moro presence. The Sultan of Sulu appeared, supported by be-turbaned dattos, and as Alice described them, "all in their best costumes: jackets seeded with pearls or beads; silk shirts of crude colors fastened at the neck with jeweled pins in gold settings; trousers of striped or slashed silk held on around the waist by heavy silk sashes, through which were stuck bolos with elaborate hilts . . ." As she viewed her surroundings—vividly garbed people against the background of Jolo's spectacular turquoise harbor—Alice felt as though a highly colored stage scene had suddenly become real.[265]

Lafayette Young observed that the U.S. Army had about twelve hundred soldiers on the tiny island, and he noted that "the Moros value human life lightly."[266] During the festivities, several hundred mounted U.S. cavalrymen, visibly armed and watchful for any sign of violence, mingled with the crowds. The beauty of the island and its warm reception of visitors merged uneasily with the sight of such a sizeable military presence.

The sultan entertained his guests with native dancers and sham battles. They were also treated to a bullfight between two ring-nosed bulls, whose philosophy seemed to be less about fighting and more "live and let live." Moro handlers prodded and pushed the bulls toward one another. They bumped heads when they couldn't avoid it and backed off when they did, at which point the handlers brought them close again and coaxed the bulls to repeat their lackadaisical performance. Such was the "bullfight."[267]

The sultan bestowed a pearl ring upon Alice, and the dattos presented her with a saddle, a bolo, and a loose pearl or two. She was delighted when they presented her with the gift of a *bobobo*, a Moro costume made up of a skirt, little jacket, and a barrel-like girdle with bells. Later aboard the *Logan*, Alice donned her Moro skirt and jacket and gave a credible performance of one of the Moro dances.[268]

Alice was quite taken with Jolo, and the sultan was taken with Alice. He asked if Alice would stay on the island, and Alice considered . . . until she was told that staying would mean becoming part of his harem. She regretfully declined.[269]

The day was hot, and the cool sea beckoned. Several of the Americans made their way to one of Jolo's beaches for a swim. One of them, Frederic O'Brien, a reporter for Cable News, Manila, was some way off the beach when a severe cramp immobilized him. Unable to swim, he was seized by a strong current, and like a scrap of flotsam, was swept relentlessly seaward. One of the congressmen, Rep. Wadsworth, took in the situation, swam to the hapless O'Brien, took him in tow and—with heroic effort—brought him into shallow water and safety.[270]

Jolo had provided the travelers with a memorable day.

4

San Francisco: Mixed Emotions

Cal McKnight stood on the deck of SS *Siberia* as the final notes of "'Til We Meet Again" trailed away. The crew cast off the dock lines, the ship moved away from its berth, and McKnight realized that the music had triggered some unsettling emotions.

Finished its task of delivering a musical farewell to a group of missionaries aboard the ship, the Salvation Army choir dispersed. The missionaries were bound for the Philippines in the service of their religion, while Cal McKnight was still trying to convince himself that he'd done the right thing by going to work for Harriman. He found that excitement over the trip was mixed with homesickness for May and Mary, the wife and daughter he wouldn't see for at least two months.[271]

A day or so earlier, once the Overland Limited had reached its terminus and the Harriman party was installed in San Francisco's Palace Hotel, McKnight had his talk with Harriman. It was not as satisfactory as he had hoped, but as good as he could expect, he thought. Harriman said he had "certain expectations" regarding McKnight, but what those expectations were, he never explained.

"Our time together will give us each a chance to decide if it would be in our mutual interest to remain together or to sever the connection when we return," Harriman said. When the conversation ended, McKnight agreed to continue on to Japan.

"He has treated me well," McKnight wrote to May.[272]

Now, as the ship transited San Francisco Bay, McKnight's thoughts churned. He wondered what Harriman's "expectations" were, and whether his work would satisfy this man who had an impatient, abrupt, and demanding reputation.

While McKnight was still absorbed in his thoughts, they passed through the Golden Gate, and he felt the ship come alive in the rolling swells of the open ocean. Each wave slowly lifted the vessel, carried it along, then dropped it, only to lift it once more and drop it again, in a relentless rhythm. Few passengers appeared for dinner that evening as "mal de mer" claimed its victims. Cal McKnight sat down bravely at his table, but service was slow, and as he waited, he asked himself doubtfully, "Do I really want anything to eat?" The answer shortly became a definite "No."

He headed abruptly to his cabin, paid his "tribute to the sea," and went straight to bed.[273]

Siberia's bow continued to rise and fall through lumpy seas as McKnight thought about Harriman. The public believed him to be a relentless acquirer with a gift for making enterprises grow. He envisioned what was necessary to enlarge the scope of the endeavor of the moment and worked out the details as he went along.

Harriman had the tenacity of a winning quarterback: weaving and dodging but always headed to the goal. Often, he simply outlasted his opponents. He had earned the lasting enmity of financier J.P. Morgan when he negotiated rights to acquire another branch line for the Illinois Central Railroad. Both men were stockholders in the branch, and Morgan had enough proxies to defeat Harriman. Harriman, however, discovered that Iowa law did not recognize proxies in stockholder meetings. The stockholder meeting was in Iowa. Harriman persuaded another stockholder to challenge the use of proxies at that meeting, citing the absence of any reference to them in Iowa law. The assembled stockholders passed the motion, and Morgan could not vote his proxies. Harriman had enough votes to carry the day. Morgan was furious and claimed that no gentleman would ever choose to win on such a technicality. Harriman was unperturbed.[274]

His enemies viewed him as one of the "robber barons," but his supporters thought of him as a good administrator who wanted his enterprises well-managed and well-maintained. Those who saw him outmaneuver J.P. Morgan described him as "ruthless," while his friends defended him as "honest and incorruptible."[275]

Harriman's father was an Episcopal rector whose gift for making money was non-existent. Orlando Harriman had failed at more than one attempt to amass some capital for his family. One thing he had done, however, was send young Edward Henry Harriman to Trinity Episcopal High School in Manhattan, a short commute from their home across the Hudson River in New Jersey.

When Harriman was fourteen, he left school and began working as a runner on Wall Street. He absorbed Wall Street's mysteries of puts, calls, and short sales, learned about corporate finance, and worked his way up into more and more responsible positions. By the time he was twenty-two he had purchased his own seat on the New York Stock Exchange and, in time, opened his own brokerage firm.[276]

In 1879, he took a step that not only charted the course of his family life but led to the passion of his working life: he married Mary Williamson Averell, daughter of a banker who was also president of an upstate New York railroad.

Mary Averell was a steady hand on the tiller of the Harriman family ship. If Henry, as she called him, was captain and navigator, then Mary Averell was executive officer. The two were very close. He respected her opinion and often consulted her.

Mary's father was young Harriman's ticket to a seat on the board of the Ogdensburg and Lake Champlain Railroad.[277] From then on, railroads became the focus for a creative energy that operated on an express schedule.

In the second half of the nineteenth century, railroad builders were like demonic quilters, stitching lines back and forth across the country. Their grasp had not always been equal to their reach, and the financial situation of many of them was shaky. Harriman saw his opportunity. Through shrewd and persistent manipulation and access to capital, he extended his holdings to control a transportation network that ranged from the Atlantic to the Pacific. By the beginning of the twentieth century, E.H. Harriman had become nationally known for restoring the Union Pacific as well as enhancing the efficiency and prosperity of a number of connecting railroads.[278]

Now, more conquests beckoned. With the conclusion of the Russo-Japanese war, a new hemisphere of possibilities presented itself. Harriman told McKnight that he expected to negotiate with the Japanese government "for the building of about a thousand miles of railroad."

Harriman emphasized that the journey would be beneficial for McKnight, even if they elected not to go on together afterward.[279] McKnight realized that no matter the outcome, throwing in his lot with Harriman meant the coming trip would be a real adventure. Even the powerful Harriman, however, couldn't foresee what lay in store.

As the ship ate up the miles to Hawaii, the wind subsided and gentler breezes drew the passengers out on deck. Except for shuffleboard, shipboard amusements were few, but when the temperature rose, the crew set up a canvas swimming pool on the upper deck. McKnight joined Harriman and his sons Roland and Averell for a plunge before breakfast.

When McKnight saw Harriman and his sons splashing in the pool together, he viewed an aspect of his new employer that didn't quite mesh with the public perception of him as grasping, manipulating, and power-hungry.[280] When he wasn't absorbed in his business activities, Harriman was absorbed in his family. He and Mary were a devoted couple. Their marriage had produced five children: Mary, Cordelia, Carol, Averell, and Roland. As the children were growing up, their father might have been fighting over control of a railroad with J.P. Morgan or secretly buying up fifty-two million dollars in Burlington stock in an attempt to extend his network in the Pacific Northwest, but he still found time to play Parcheesi, dominoes, or backgammon with them in the evening.[281]

Young Mary Harriman's friend, Alice Roosevelt, described Harriman as "a small, brown, taciturn man who never seemed to play—that nothing he did was ever 'just for fun.' But he always had a twinkle in his eye with his children, who were devoted to him, and he certainly did let them play . . ."[282]

Once this relaxing shipboard interlude ended and the real work of the trip began, Harriman would not be dealing with subordinates or his fellow financiers. In his give-and-take with Japanese officials, he'd face individuals from a different culture at the highest level of government.

McKnight realized that Harriman was right about the job. It could be interesting and, as events played out, memorable.

5

Oyster Bay: Sticking Points

Theodore Roosevelt always relished his time at Sagamore Hill, but the summer of 1905 was trying. He had managed to bring delegates from Russia and Japan together so that they could shape a peace settlement to a war that neither country could afford.

The president, however, was not privy to the actual negotiations. His fellow Harvard graduate, Baron Kaneko, was in close communication with the Japanese delegation and kept Roosevelt informed about progress or lack thereof in the deliberations.

What Roosevelt was hearing was not encouraging.[283]

The principal negotiators, Witte for Russia and Komura for Japan, had arrived by sea in Portsmouth, New Hampshire. They and their retinues moved into the Wentworth Hotel, an enormous frame structure that accommodated well-to-do visitors from the Northeast's sweltering cities. Each day, the two men emerged to ride by motorcar to the naval stores building at the Portsmouth Naval Shipyard.[284]

The Japanese had arrived in Portsmouth with a list of demands to which their government thought they were entitled, because their forces had been victors over both the Russian army and navy. The Russians knew that the Japanese army was not in control of any part of mainland Russia, and the Russian army at Mukden had not surrendered. Their position was strong, and they were not going to give in easily to Japanese demands.[285]

Experienced negotiators rarely believe they will get all they ask for. They expect to concede on the points less important to them in order to prevail on the points that mean the most. On August 10, Baron Komura had presented Japan's terms.[286] Count Witte kept his staff up until one the next morning preparing the Russian response.[287] The two sides debated for hours over each proposal. Even when they agreed, Komura would persist until the wording was precise, a challenging task, as the Japanese spoke English and the Russians spoke French.[288]

After several intense days, the two sides agreed on provisions relating to Korea. And in Manchuria, Japan would receive Port Arthur, the southern section of the Manchurian Railway, and the lease on the Liaotung Peninsula. So far, so good.[289]

They disposed of other, less crucial problems, but on two issues they were oceans apart: Japan's government insisted on a payment of reparations and the cession of more significant territory. Tsar Nicholas announced that he would never, ever, give up any land nor hand over any money to the Japanese. That would be his stance until the end, he declared.[290]

Following previous wars in the Far East, the victor had traditionally received reparations from the vanquished. Thus, many Japanese citizens believed a monetary settlement to be their just due. Some also believed the Russians had unfairly deprived them of Sakhalin Island when they took it in exchange for the Kurile Islands in 1875. Komura took a hard line. Witte continued to forcefully state his opposition to reparations, while repeating that the tsar had forbidden him to discuss ceding Sakhalin.[291]

Five hundred mountainous miles long, Sakhalin lies north of the Japanese island of Hokkaido and parallels the Russian coast to the west. Across the Perouse Strait, Sakhalin is visible from Japan, and can be seen from mainland Russia across the Tartar Strait. Each country regarded the island as an extension of its own territory.

Fish and whales abound in Sakhalin's surrounding seas. But although mushrooms and wild berries grow abundantly, the land is not particularly suited for crop farming. Reindeer roam, snow abounds, and summer is short. Japanese fishermen had been taking from the fertile waters off the southeast coast since the late eighteenth century, and Russians had settled the northern portion beginning a half-century before.[292]

The first armed confrontations between Russia and Japan occurred in 1806 and 1807. For several years in the mid-nineteenth century, both nations shared governance of the island. Then, in 1875, the Russians gained control of Sakhalin in exchange for the nearby Kurile Islands. But Sakhalin continued to be a disputed piece of territory, the rope in a never-ending tug-of-war.

And now, Sakhalin looked to be the block of lead that could sink the peace process. Both Komura and Witte were achingly aware of their countries' situations: they knew carrying on the war would be financially disastrous. In Russia, anti-government sentiment roiled, and Witte believed that securing peace was essential for the government to survive.[293]

The biggest obstacle to a settlement, however, was Tsar Nicholas himself. He was a man easily swayed by the opinions of his advisors. And, as many weak men do, he displayed a streak of iron on certain subjects. Sakhalin was one of them. Nicholas believed he ruled by divine command, and therefore was responsible for the "honor of Russia." Thus, to cede territory would be dishonoring his country. The tsar's word was law, and on the subject of Sakhalin, the tsar was immovable.[294]

In the heat of that summer in Oyster Bay, Roosevelt weighed the information he continued to receive about the situation in Portsmouth and concluded that he would have to take action.

Cables flew across both Atlantic and Pacific oceans as Roosevelt pressured leaders of other nations to urge the Japanese government and the Russian tsar to prepare to accept a compromise.

He was in particularly close communication with the U.S. ambassador to St. Petersburg, George von Lengerke Meyer, the man who had prevailed upon the tsar to send his representative to the negotiations.

If Tsar Nicholas were going to agree to compromise, Meyer would have to do the persuading.

6
Islands: Mindanao to Luzon

Until now, the travelers had visited among friendly people, even on Jolo. But not so in Mindanao. Indigenous tribes living there and on the islands of the Sulu archipelago had converted to Islam before the Spanish arrived in the 1500s. The Moros did not appreciate Spanish attempts to control them, and since then, the tribes had been in a chronic state of rebellion.

When the U.S. took over the Philippines at the end of the war with Spain, the Moros did not stop fighting. Frances Pershing's husband, John, then a captain, led a U.S. Army contingent sent to subdue the Moros. He won over most of them by convincing them that the Americans were not going to change their religion but wanted only to end the fighting. Only those few he was unable to peacefully persuade did he subdue by military action.[295]

On the way to Mindanao, the Taft mission had progressed from Manila, on the island of Luzon, to coastal settlements on the islands of Panay and Negros, and on to the islands of Mindanao and Jolo. From Jolo they returned to Mindanao, the second largest island in the Philippines. The plan was to venture inland from Malabang on Mindanao's south coast across a narrow neck of land to Camp Overton on the north coast, with a stop at the army camp in the highlands near Lake Lanao.

Some of the party chose to proceed in carriages, but others—including Secretary Taft and Alice—opted to ride on horseback. "It was my first opportunity to use the sidesaddle" (Alice had brought her own saddle all the way from the States) "only to find that the girths would not fit any of the animals provided. So there and then it was discarded and I rode the trail on an army saddle, my [riding] habit very much in the way."[296]

The trail led upward amidst thickets of vegetation, monster ferns lifting their fronds skyward, monkeys flitting sporadically through trees lashed with vines as thick as tugboat hawsers, the sky only sometimes visible, and the ever-present mud-filled ruts sucking the horses in up to their knees.

The road was barely worthy of the name, but the jungle seemed to resent its presence and tried to demolish it. Because this was Moro country, cavalry troops preceded the travelers to protect them. As it turned out, they saw only one Moro settlement of small grass huts and no Moros in the flesh.

Hours of tedious progress finally led them to the high, undulating plains that surrounded the army's Camp Vickers. There, grasses eight or ten feet tall sprouted from the black volcanic soil. Beyond the camp, the travelers abandoned wagons and horses to scramble down a precipitous, muddy path to the expanse of Lake Lanao itself.[297]

When John Pershing was transferred out of Mindanao, his horse remained at Camp Vickers. For this trek, his wife, Frances, was riding her husband's horse. Before she dismounted, two young Moro teenagers who recognized the horse rushed up to Frances.

"John Pershing is our father!" they proclaimed at the top of their voices to a thoroughly disconcerted Frances Pershing. Only weeks later was John Pershing finally able to explain.

"The boy was the son of a Moro, Datto Ahmai Tampgao, and the girl the daughter of Sultan Ganassi, both of whom were particular friends of mine and who, according to Moro custom, had honored me by asking me to adopt their children. I had become their honorary father."[298]

To reach Camp Keithley, their destination for the night, the travelers needed to cross Lake Lanao and sail eastward along its northern shore. The lake was beautiful, rimmed with mountains but reflecting the dark clouds that menaced overhead.

The little flotilla kept moving purposefully, hoping to outrun the storm. Night fell as somber clouds cast a threatening aura over their small boats. It grew darker still until, finally, the storm burst. Rain poured in torrents, and when the party spilled out of the boats at Camp Keithley, they were drenched and shivering in sixty-degree temperatures.

The camp officers' families hospitably took them in, helped them dry off, and sheltered them for the night in homes built of bamboo and grass with long rolls of thatching covering the glass-free windows. Awakened by morning light that shone through gaps in the siding, Alice and Mabel Boardman pushed up their window coverings.

"[We] felt ourselves in quite a Robinson Crusoe atmosphere," Mabel marveled.

As they left the camp in the hazy dawn, they could see the shimmering lake on one side and, in the distance, the expanse of the ocean. They still had eighteen miles of military "road" to negotiate, twelve miles of it constructed of bamboo corduroy, more absent than present. Once again, the horses struggled through mud to their knees while the wagons were hub-deep in ruts. After hours of full-body abuse, the travelers reached yet another military post, Camp Overton on the shores of Illigan Bay, and eventually, *Logan*'s comforts.[299]

The travelers could cross off their lists the islands of Panay, Negros, Jolo, and Mindanao (twice). Ahead of them were visits to Cebu, Leyte, and tiny Maclan, before their circle tour ended back on Luzon, from whence they'd started.

Cebu was first. There, a poor rice crop and touches of famine had left the people forlorn. Nevertheless, the islanders greeted the travelers with decorations, a parade, a banquet, and a ball. The party met two American women who were the only nurses in the tiny hospital where they treated sick women and children. Doctors were in short supply throughout the Philippines, but many Filipinos were studying medicine in the States in order to return to the Philippines to serve.[300]

Reports were that, on the southern islands, more than $100,000 had been spent on entertaining the visiting Americans. Lafayette Young noted that "a number of members of Congress were unhappy because they knew the people were spending money which they could not afford."

Young was diligent in his pursuit of economic information. He was particularly impressed with the local fabrics made from the fiber of hemp and pineapple, some of it "fine as silk." He'd investigated the potential profitability of growing hemp and rice and concluded that the islands' economic potential was positive.[301]

For the Americans, only a few days of their island tour remained. Aboard *Logan* again, they left Cebu and made a brief stop at the city of Tacloban on the island of Leyte. There, they found the residents cheerfully enjoying prosperity fueled by a successful hemp crop. Then, in small boats once more, the travelers transited the very narrow Straits of San Jacinto between the islands of Samar and Leyte, through placid, protected waters, their sails filled with soft tropic winds.[302]

They could be serene in the belief that they had done their duty by meeting the Filipinos on their home grounds. They came, they saw, they listened. Nevertheless, with her sociologist's eye and a strong interest in native culture wherever she found it, Elsie Parsons noted that the junketers did not socialize with the indigenous population, but instead spent their time mainly with the Spanish and Americans. She believed this contrasted with Taft's custom of hosting people from all segments of the population when he was governor.[303]

Now, in the grand sightseeing tradition, one intrepid group from the *Logan* went on to view the monument erected by the Spanish in honor of Ferdinand Magellan. The site of Magellan's death on the island of Maclan was remote. The sightseers packed themselves into small boats once again, but when they approached the land, the water was so thin over the bottom that even the small boats could not make it to shore. Natives carried the two women in the party to dry land, but the men were forced to splash through the shallows, some of them barefoot, probably in the identical fashion that Magellan himself first reached the island.[304]

Ferdinand Magellan is thought of as the first man to circumnavigate the globe, but on his final voyage, Magellan himself reached only as far as the Philippines. There he made the mistake of getting involved in local politics. He had sailed from Spain to the southern tip of South America, discovered the passage to the Pacific later known as the Straits of Magellan, crossed the Pacific to the Marianas, and with his ships and several hundred men, eventually arrived on the Philippine island of Cebu.

Magellan became friends with a local chief, Rajah Humadon, and his wife, both of whom looked kindly on the Spaniards, embraced Christianity, and allowed themselves to be baptized. Then Rajah Humadon asked Magellan to kill his enemy, Lapu Lapu. First, Magellan tried to convert Lapu Lapu to Christianity, but Lapu Lapu would have none of it. A fierce battle followed. A spear took Magellan down, and Lapu Lapu's men swarmed around him and dealt the blows that killed him and others of the crew.

Juan Sebastian Elcano, captain of Magellan's ship *Victoria*, escaped and continued eastward. Three years after Magellan and his five ships left Spain, Elcano captained the only ship to complete the voyage. Of the original crew, only nineteen men returned to Spain.

In a beautiful grove of palm trees, the crumbling monument, placed by the Spanish almost two centuries earlier, marked (and presumably still marks) the place where Magellan lost his life on April 27, 1521. He had once sailed east from Spain to Southeast Asia, so technically he *had* been around the world once, but on two different ships and in two different directions.

ↀ

On a cloudless morning, the Taft party left Cebu and sailed north to reach the southernmost part of Luzon, the island from which their tour had begun. Mount Mayon towered in volcanic majesty nine thousand feet above the sea and provided a dramatic backdrop for the beginning of the end of their two-week tour.[305] After a difficult landing at Legaspi—*Logan* had to anchor eight miles out—Secretary Taft had one final task: he was to dedicate a new bridge at nearby Sorsogon. The secretary delivered appropriate remarks, including, "I name this bridge 'The Alice Roosevelt Bridge,' and I hope it may stand to accommodate Miss Roosevelt's children and grandchildren."

Alice was sitting in the audience and was observed to blush and hang her head.[306] She could console herself, however, with the thought that she easily could be the world's only living twenty-one-year-old woman who had a bridge named for her.

After another twenty-four hours aboard the *Logan*, they were back in Manila once more, amidst a sea of farewell social events. For their final days in the Philippines, Alice stayed in the home of Commissioner Legardo, a member of the presidential commission. After a month among the islands, she should have begun to feel at home, but a curious experience reminded her that she was in the midst of a different culture.

"I had a great big room, in a corner of which a little staircase let down most unexpectedly through a square hole in the floor. Out of that opening, at odd hours of the day and night, small Filipino heads would suddenly pop up like prairie dogs, look at me with much interest, and then disappear again."[307]

The tide of farewell parties ebbed, and on August 31, Secretary Taft, the congressional delegation, their wives, Alice, Frances Pershing, Mabel Boardman, Amy McMillan, Gen. and Mrs. Corbin, Lafayette Young, and the others, boarded their ship and happily headed for Hong Kong, for a brief taste of what life was like in an outpost of the British Empire.

P. M. S. S. Co's "Siberia".

Aug. 19 – 1905

Dearest Little Angel:

Daddy sends you a whole lot of kisses and lots and lots of love. Be a good little girl until "Daddy" comes home. Kiss Mamma and give her a good hug for Daddy. Your old Daddy

A letter from Cal McKnight to his young daughter, Mary, highlights the homesickness he grappled with while embarking on the months-long voyage aboard SS Siberia. Attached to a picture of the vessel, McKnight wrote to Mary:

Dearest Little Angel,
Daddy sends you a whole lot of kisses and lots and lots of love. Be a good little girl until "Daddy" comes home. Kiss Mamma and give her a good hug for Daddy.

—Your old Daddy

One of two Japanese elder statesmen, Marquis Hirobumi Ito met with Harriman in September 1905 to discuss ideas regarding the future of Manchuria Railways. As a powerful decision maker, Ito played an important role in modernizing Asian railroad travel with Western-style luxuries.

Empress Cixi, widower of China's late Prince Ching, had an affinity for Pekingese dogs. As one of her many offerings, Empress Cixi gifted Alice her own black Pekingese, whom she named Manchu as a tribute to the country's last imperial dynasty.

Harriman chartered the USS Ohio III to transport his entourage safely from Kyoto to the naval base Port Arthur in order to get a first-hand look at the Manchurian Railways.

Along with several Korean officials, Minister Morgan and Willard Straight met Alice and her companions upon their arrival in Chemulpo, Korea. With the majority of her emissarial assignments completed, Alice's principal duty was to simply respond to the hospitality of the Korean emperor and Japanese officials.

From garden parties with government officials to luncheons with cabinet ministers, Harriman's visit to Tokyo was a warmly welcomed event, despite the secrecy, speculation and ambiguity that was surrounding the railway treaty signing.

7

Midway and Hawaii: Island Pleasures

With both the line's owner and its managing director aboard, the captain pushed *Siberia* without mercy. The speed record between San Francisco and Honolulu was at stake.[308]

Five days out of San Francisco, *Siberia* and its passengers were still thousands of miles away from the Far East, but Hawaii's lively volcano Kilauea (called Mt. Pele by Hawaiians) loomed over the horizon. Honolulu's harbor soon opened up, framed by palm and banana trees. The passengers learned that *Siberia* had outdone itself and now held the record for the fastest passage ever between San Francisco and Honolulu.

While the ship maneuvered toward the dock, passengers tossed pennies into the crystal-clear water below. The local boys, graceful as tropical fish and as much at home in the water as on the land, swam to the bottom to retrieve them. As soon as the gangway was lowered, McKnight dashed off to the cable company office to dispatch and receive messages.

Then the party was off to a day of sightseeing on this island that had been a U.S. territory for only five years, since U.S. sugar interests had persuaded President William McKinley to annex it after the same interests played a major role in deposing Queen Liliuokalani.[309]

Since the early 1800s, whalers had been using Honolulu's port to restock their ships, traders had used it as a waystation, and unsuccessful gold miners had come for the easy living. Missionaries had long been a major presence. Americans were no strangers to the islands, but twenty more years would pass before tourism took hold. Meanwhile, what McKnight saw was an island influenced by Americans but still with its authentic character intact. He found the Polynesian women in their missionary-decreed Mother Hubbards (long, shapeless cotton dresses) both "good-looking and intelligent" while the men were "straight as arrows, with clean-cut . . . cameo features."

McKnight and the Harrimans spent the afternoon at Nakela Beach. Like Alice Roosevelt and her friends a few weeks before, they found themselves completely captivated by the island's signature sport: surfing. In a letter to his wife, McKnight described the scene:

> There is a fine surf, much better than anything on the Atlantic Coast that I have ever seen. The water is warm and the beach fine sand, but the real sport is in riding the surf in canoes and on surf boards. The canoes are about twenty feet long and hold six people. You go out about a half-mile from shore and wait until you see a big roller coming in. The Kanaka boy who does the steering with an oar from the stern gives the word to paddle and everyone paddles as hard as possible. Then, if the roller catches you right . . . away you go like the wind, with the water flying over you and blinding you. It carries you to the beach . . . in about a minute.
>
> The skill of the oarsman keeps the boat straight. If she should swing around in front of the breaker she would almost certainly be swamped. Coming in on one of the rollers our steersman lost his oar. In a second we had been thrown broadside to the wave and shipped a boatful of water before we could straighten her out. Fortunately, we had gotten pretty well to shore and got her into shallow water before she sank. We put in all afternoon in the ca-

> noe and bathing and I tell you it was the most exhilarating sport that I have ever had.[310]

That evening, while *Siberia* was preparing to pull away from the dock, a Japanese string band serenaded the departing passengers. No one was safe from Hawaiians armed with festoons of exotic flowers seeking to bedeck their departing friends. As if dispensed by a florist gone berserk, long colorful circlets of blooms draped shoulders and hats in every direction. The travelers enjoyed their island farewell.

With its passengers safely aboard, the crew cast off the lines and the ship worked its way down the harbor, as the lilt of Polynesian singing drifted through the darkness.[311] The music grew fainter until the *Siberia* finally put Honolulu firmly astern and steamed into the open Pacific.

They left the southeastern, mountainous tip of a thousand-mile-long, largely underwater, archipelago and headed to Midway Island, at the northwest end of the chain.

Siberia's captain approached the island cautiously, doubtless aware that sudden and severe storms had struck Midway and brought many a ship to grief on the treacherous coral outcroppings that lie just beneath the surface. At six in the morning, the captain ordered *Siberia*'s anchor dropped about four miles offshore. Hardly had the anchor's splash subsided than small boats approached. They bore employees of the Pacific Commercial Cable Company and a party of U.S. Marines, who arrived at the foot of the gangway to pick up their incoming mail.

By eight o'clock, Captain Smith ordered three of the ship's boats lowered. The captain himself led the shore party, which included only E. H. Harriman, his children, and McKnight. Six Chinese crewmen pulled the oars in each boat, and they headed toward what looked to be a desert island. McKnight enjoyed being transported through the blue-green water to what had until recently been an uninhabited speck in the Pacific Ocean.[312] Although the U.S. had claimed possession of the sparsely vegetated sandy outcropping for more than thirty years, Theodore Roosevelt had given responsibility for it to the U.S. Navy only two years before. That same year, employees of the cable company arrived. Although shipwreck victims had taken brief refuge there, the cable company's people could claim to be Midway's first settlers. The settlers were first in another way as well: their underwater cable station was a link in the planet's first 'round-the-world communication circuit.

The boats eased their way through the narrow opening in the reef and into the quieter waters inside, where the islanders—including a company of twenty U.S. Marines—gave them an enthusiastic welcome. Midway was not on any regular ship route, and the island's only human callers came by way of occasional stops by the cable-laying steamer or the odd military transport.

At the time of *Siberia*'s arrival, the inhabitants had received no mail for 106 days. Worse still, some months earlier, they had come close to starvation. McKnight explained in a letter to May: "The boats from a ship which had arrived with provisions could not get in because of rough weather. The people had to live on fish for several months. In April a storm swept over the island, washed away their boats, and left them in a generally wrecked condition."

The wife of the cable crew's superintendent was the first woman ever to land on the island. Young Mary, Cornelia, and Carol Harriman were the second, third, and fourth.

From Midway, McKnight cabled his wife, "It impressed me as simply marvelous away out here in the Pacific to be in touch with home. We sent a message to San Francisco [thousands of] miles away and received a reply in fifteen minutes."

When it was time to return to *Siberia*, a favorable wind inspired the crew to hoist the sails of the two smaller boats. Sails full, the boats raced each other back to the ship.

While they'd been ashore, several Chinese crewmen had passed the time fishing. Just as the passengers were starting up the gangplank, one of the fishermen landed a six-foot shark, adding a final fillip of excitement to the day.[313]

The crew raised the anchor and Midway soon fell over the horizon behind them.

Eleven days would pass before they'd see land again.

8

Portsmouth: Reluctant Compromise

"Peace!"

The word blared from the phone's earpiece.

A clutch of press correspondents from London, Rome, Paris, Frankfurt, St. Petersburg, and Tokyo were huddled in the Hotel Wentworth's lobby. On the line was the secretary to the chief of the Russian delegation, who excitedly conveyed the message that Russia and Japan had agreed upon terms for a treaty to end the most destructive war the world had ever seen. [314]

Until then, reporters (and the negotiators themselves) had believed that the peace conference was doomed to founder on the rocks of Japanese hardheadedness and Russian intransigence. After three weeks of negotiations, the Russian representative, Witte, had been ordered home by the tsar.[315] Baron Jutaro Komura, Japan's chief negotiator, had packed his bags and settled his hotel bill.[316] But no one departed.

Although Roosevelt never again met the delegates after he'd introduced them, he was in almost constant communication with ambassadors, foreign ministers, and heads of state in France, Germany, England, Russia, and Japan, bringing to bear all the influence he could muster to persuade the two sides to come to an agreement.[317] The mantra of these European governments was "balance of power." They wanted a peace that would restrain both nations.[318]

Because they'd broken the siege at Port Arthur, defeated the Russian army at Mukden, and wiped out the Russian fleet at Tsu Shima, the Japanese thought they'd won the war. But, even after the battle at Mukden, the Russian army was intact and, in spite of heavy casualties, was able to retreat to the north. The tsar enjoyed the illusion that Russia had not really lost. He believed that Russia had enough money and men to continue the fight. Meanwhile, the Japanese were running out of money and had made no military moves other than to occupy the poorly defended island of Sakhalin. Neither side felt the need to move off its position.

Komura was obdurate on the issues of reparations and Sakhalin. Witte was not shy about opposing reparations, and the tsar had forbidden him to talk about ceding Sakhalin.[319] By mid-August, both negotiators believed that the conference was about to end without resolution. The two sides were reduced to sitting across the table from each other in silence for up to eight minutes at a time.[320]

Then the tsar ordered Count Witte to return home. As finance minister, Witte believed that the war's continuation could completely de-stabilize an already shaky Russian regime. He was in no hurry to return home without an agreement.[321] He was subject to the tsar's orders but did not rush to pack his suitcase.

Meanwhile, Roosevelt was busy behind the scenes communicating with the tsar through the U.S. ambassador to Russia, George von Lengerke Meyer.[322] If diplomacy can be called the art of persuading others to accept the unacceptable, Meyer was a hard-working practitioner. Formerly ambassador to Italy, he had only recently been appointed to the St. Petersburg post, but it was he who had convinced the tsar to participate in the peace conference in the first place. Meyer went to work again. He spent hours in conversation with the tsar, who was unwilling to accept any conditions that would imply defeat of the motherland. In particular, he would not concede Sakhalin Island, even though the Japanese were occupying it. The word "reparations" was still anathema.[323] Roosevelt refused to give up. He had received a hint that the Russians might be willing to accept a Japanese commercial presence on Sakhalin.[324] Within hours, Meyer presented the tsar with Roosevelt's suggestion for a compromise. It would be a Russian face-saver while satisfying the Japanese belief that they were entitled to both land and money. The island of Sakhalin would be divided: Japan would retain the territory south of the fiftieth parallel, and Russia would purchase the northern half from Japan. The payment would not be called "reparations," but whatever it was called, the money would go to the Japanese treasury.

Despite hours of face-to-face conversation with the tsar, Meyer could not persuade him to pay for Sakhalin. It took several hours to get an agreement that Russia would pay for maintenance of Russian prisoners of war held by the Japanese. Pushing further, Meyer finally received the grudging concession that Japan could keep a portion of Sakhalin.[325]

Roosevelt fired a fusillade of cables pressuring the Japanese to accept the compromise. Continuing the war would cost Japan more in a year than the loss of the indemnity, he emphasized.[326]

Peace negotiations reached a crisis state.

The negotiating session on August 29 was scheduled to be the last. The two negotiators faced each other across the table. Witte spoke first. His country offered one (and only one) concession: Russia would cede the southern half of the island of Sakhalin to the Japanese.

Komura answered that Japan was prepared to give up its demand for an indemnity if it received all of Sakhalin.

"No," Witte responded flatly.

The room was quiet . . . and the quiet went on . . . and on . . . and on . . .

Bits of paper dropped to the table as Witte steadily pulled apart a discarded note. Tension reigned.

Finally, the unemotional Komura spoke. Because peace was desirable, he indicated, Japan would do without an indemnity and would share a divided Sakhalin Island with Russia.[327]

For better or worse, the Treaty of Portsmouth would become a reality.

PART VI

RIOTS AND ROYALTY

September 1905

1

Yokohama: Colorful Evening

From *Siberia*'s deck, all Cal McKnight could glimpse were the ghostly shadows of other ships in limbo. In the eleven days since their departure from Midway, *Siberia*'s passengers had seen neither ship nor land. They were eager to go ashore but had just been told that they couldn't go until the next day. To deepen their frustration, fog and haze had drawn an opaque curtain between ship and shore.

Because *Siberia* drew too much water to be accommodated dockside, the captain had ordered the anchor dropped about three-quarters of a mile from shore. Fifty-one years earlier, Commodore Matthew Perry in his flagship, the USS *Powhatan*, had anchored in the same stretch of water in order to conclude the negotiations that produced the 1854 treaty that first allowed American ships to enter Japanese ports. At the time that Perry arrived, Japan was still governed by the Tokugawa family, last of the military shogun rulers who had governed Japan for more than 250 years. The shoguns' legacy included a 1639 law that forbade Japanese people to travel abroad and barred foreigners from visiting Japan.[328]

In the 1860s, a British minister to Tokyo, Sir Rutherford Alcock, commented, "The Japanese allow no distinction of nationalities to stand between them and their one object, which is the expulsion of foreigners and a return to their isolation. Their distrust of foreign powers is indiscriminate, and their hatred perfectly impartial."[329]

The treaty with the U.S. was a major step in Japan's emergence from its feudal isolation. Japanese leaders began to be exposed to Western ways of doing things.[330] By 1868, opposition to the existing government had grown strong enough to overthrow the last of the Tokugawas, restore the Meiji emperor (Mikado) to power, and establish him in Tokyo. Though ostensibly democratic after 1869, in practice the country was governed by an alliance of nobles and former military leaders who could trace their lineage back to the samurai, the feudal warrior caste.[331]

The governing alliance set to work to modernize Japan, modeling its institutions after what they saw as the most successful ones in the West. When they established the compulsory education system, they consulted the French; when restructuring their army, they looked to the Prussians; for a model for their navy, they turned to the British.

They believed that transforming the Japanese economy from an agrarian to an industrial one was crucial. They invited Western experts to teach in Japan; Japanese students were sent to foreign countries to learn languages and business methods.[332] By the time of *Siberia*'s arrival, the days of Japanese opposition to foreigners seemed to be as out of date as a samurai sword. Yokohama welcomed the Americans in a way that would have astonished Commodore Perry.

As soon as *Siberia*'s anchor line was taut, the sampan fleet, which had been visible for some time, surrounded the ship. Each of these small boats was operated by two men, naked except for breech clouts, steering and propelling by means of a long scull over the side or stern. "The way they go through the water is a caution," McKnight marveled. What really impressed him, however, was the volume of noise created by the voices of the sampan boatmen competing for the business of taking passengers and their luggage ashore. "The noise they made would have driven ten thousand parrots mad from envy," McKnight wrote in a letter to his wife May later that day.[333]

Visitors swarmed aboard to greet Harriman. First on hand were Pacific Mail officials who arrived in a company launch. Next were Japanese government officials who came to extend invitations to luncheons, dinners, and garden parties in Tokyo. They immediately shared the news that the peace treaty ending Japan's war with Russia had been signed, although its terms had not yet been made public.

McKnight noted:

As yet, strict censorship of the government had prevented any leaking out of news concerning the treaty of peace with Russia, although one of the government officials with whom I spoke admitted that they expected the treaty to be signed soon. As a matter-of-fact that very minute it had already been signed for more than twenty-four hours, but its terms were such that the government feared to make them public at that time.[334]

Peace treaty or no, the visiting Americans were in the grip of that excitement that bubbles up when an exotic locale first presents itself. They were anxious to absorb the sights, smells, and sounds of this place, so different from all they knew. To their pleasant surprise, the Japanese customs officials who came aboard cleared the members of the Harriman group to go ashore immediately. A Pacific Mail launch came alongside *Siberia*, took on the entire party, and, just at dark, deposited them on the pier ashore. There, rickshaws were waiting to take them to the Grand Hotel. Each of these two-wheeled carriages carried one person and was pulled by a Japanese man between the shafts. "The endurance of these fellows is remarkable," McKnight noted in a letter to his wife. "They go along at a trot and will keep going for hours without apparent fatigue. It costs twenty *sen* (ten cents) an hour or two *yen* by the day, equal to fifty cents, American."

As they were whisked through the busy streets for dinner at the Grand Hotel, the day was drawing to a close. After dinner, the travelers were out on the streets once more. In his letter to May, McKnight continued:

> . . . the lantern-lighted and busy streets, glimpses of which we had caught on our way to the hotel, beckoned

> to us and called with an irresistible voice. So [we] were soon in rickshaws winding in and out of the quaint little streets . . . among a quaint and picturesque little people in a city of miniature houses.
>
> That first sight of a Japanese city can never be forgotten by a Westerner. What he sees—from the people to their homes, from their dress to their manners and their workshops—is so entirely different from anything at home, that the first impression is sure to be a lasting one . . . One seems to be stepping back in time . . .

The narrow streets were without sidewalks and teemed with people who were much shorter than Americans, as McKnight had expected. "[B]ut they are so compactly, solidly, and athletically built that one loses the idea of smallness . . ."

McKnight observed that a Japanese man was occasionally seen in Western clothing but a woman, never. All of the women and children and the majority of men were dressed in cotton robes draped gracefully about them and with slits that showed their legs almost to the hips. The coolies (laborers) wore a cotton shirt and a breech clout.

McKnight was totally charmed by the infants, and found them to be cute, pretty little dolls who reminded him of the images in Christmas windows on 23rd Street or 6th Avenue (New York). To him, the rainbow colors harmonized because "the Japanese were artists at combining colors so they didn't offend the eye as if they were used by an Englishman or American."

Harriman may have come to Japan on railroad business, but the next day his family and fellow travelers were shopping, drawn by shop windows displaying works of art in metal, clay, or fabric. They learned to bargain and stayed to buy. McKnight marveled at the prices that were a third of what they would have been in New York. He had a suit made between nine in the morning and three that same afternoon for thirty-two *yen* (sixteen dollars) and bought half-a-dozen shirts for twelve *yen* (about six dollars).[335]

But it was time to move on. Before they left Yokohama, a representative of the president of the Bank of Japan had appeared. Representatives of other banks, as well as Japan's minister of finance, railroad presidents, the American consul in Yokohama, a U.S. Navy surgeon, and officials of the Standard Oil Company and the Equitable Life Insurance Company all appeared at the Grand Hotel to pay their respects to E. H. Harriman. Count K. Inouye had called, and Harriman even received a note from the chairman of the Japan Central Board Tea Traders' Guild.[336]

And this was just the beginning.

2

Tokyo: Discontented Rumblings

The treaty had been signed, but as yet the public had no idea of what it said. Strict censorship hid the precise terms of the treaty from the press, but drifting like smoke from a faraway fire, a sense grew among the population that the peace treaty was not the treaty they deserved after their sacrifice of men and treasure.

On September 3, the Harriman party arrived in Tokyo aboard a special train provided for the thirty-minute journey from Yokohama. On their way from the station to the American legation, McKnight saw placards prominently displayed everywhere.

"What do they say?" he asked their interpreter. The interpreter explained that the Anti-Peace Society was urging the public to come to Hibiya Park on September 5, two days later, to protest the signing of the treaty.[337] Segments of the press were critical of what they knew of the treaty and had hung flags of black crepe at their offices. (Baroness d'Anethan, wife of the Belgian ambassador to Japan, commented in her diary entry of September 3, "The Japanese Press has quite lost its head, publishing caricatures of Marquis Katsura and Baron Komura surrounded by skulls, skeletons, and other ghastly . . . objects.")[338]

The public had not an inkling of the obstacles that Japan's delegate Komura had faced at the peace conference. The Japanese man-in-the-street had no way to know of the tsar's inability to accept his army and navy's poor performance against what Russians thought of as a minor Far Eastern nation. The public knew nothing of the tsar's refusal to cede Sakhalin. They didn't know that Russia's ruler believed Russia could continue to fight the Japanese army. And the Japanese government had not reported publicly that its own army's supply lines in Manchuria were seriously overstretched, nor that the government's financial position was precarious. The public's expectations of an indemnity and the ownership of the whole of Sakhalin had not been met. Many Japanese felt their country had won the war but lost the peace.

Meanwhile, the Griscoms invited the Harriman family to stay at the U.S. legation, while the remainder of the party went to the Imperial Hotel.[339] The Americans were intrigued by Japanese culture but were unwilling to set aside their familiar comforts for it. The Imperial Hotel supplied them with what they expected: Western-style comforts and meals. From the hotel they'd have a view of Hibiya Park across the street, an oasis of greenery, flowering trees, azaleas, and chrysanthemums.

Rumors about the terms of the treaty were flying, and what the populace was hearing was not what they had expected. Emotions ran high, but facts were lacking. In the meantime, on the evening of September 4, Lloyd and Elsa Griscom entertained at a dinner for their guests. The Griscoms had also invited cabinet ministers and government officials, which gave E.H. Harriman a splendid opportunity to meet Japanese officialdom with decision-making powers relevant to the Manchurian railways.[340] The ministers came face to face with an E.H. Harriman who had fixed squarely upon a goal. He would use his intensely focused powers of persuasion to bring their ideas about the future of Manchuria's railways in line with his own plans.

Two of the country's four living elder statesmen were present: Marquis Ito and Count Inouye. Griscom's neighbor, Hirobumi Ito, was president of the nation's privy council and advisor to the emperor. As a former prime minister, he was a figure known world-wide. Ito had once been wary of foreigners, but travel and study in Europe had shifted his convictions completely: the name of Marquis Hirobumi Ito was now tied to the ideas of modernization.

Also on hand were Count Katsura, the current prime minister, and other members of the emperor's cabinet, including Mr. Watanbe, Lord of Ceremonies, and Viscount Tanaka, Minister for the Imperial Household. All of the officials of the American legation and their wives were present, including military attaché John Pershing. E. H. Harriman was seated next to Mrs. Arthur MacArthur, Jr., the wife of the general who was serving with Pershing as a military observer of the war, and whose son, Douglas, only a few years out of West Point, was also serving in the Far East.

The Griscoms' party-hosting skills were evidenced not only by the number of the country's decision-makers in attendance, but by the sparkle they'd added to the lackluster legation quarters with elegant linens, crystal, and china. "It was a gorgeous affair," McKnight wrote to his wife.

After dinner, the guests adjourned to the parlors where the men—and the Japanese women—smoked. As he talked with these men at the top layers of government (several of whom spoke English), McKnight discovered that they shared feelings of foreboding about the way the public was receiving news of the peace treaty. He was told that some newspapers were openly urging for members of the peace delegation to be murdered. McKnight felt the officials displayed impressive composure in the face of their anxieties. [341]

The Japanese had sacrificed much in the way of treasure, both human and material, to win the war's major battles. Harriman's friend Jacob Schiff had helped Japanese bankers float the bonds that helped to finance the war against Russia. Harriman's potential financial participation was of tremendous interest to those responsible for Japan's recovery from the financial stress of the war.

As he strove to establish a working relationship with these Japanese power-wielders, Harriman responded to a toast by saying that the Japanese would enjoy material prosperity more quickly if they "realized the advantages which follow concentration of effort and harmony of operation in their industrial and commercial affairs." He went on the describe the "incalculable" benefits of having ten thousand miles of railroad and steamship lines under one management, and expressed his hope that Japanese and American businessmen, aware of their "common interest," would soon be working together. [342]

The events of the next few days would challenge his audience, both Japanese and American.

3

Canton and Hong Kong: Distant Views

Canton was different. No princesses waited to greet them with flowers, no bands paraded, and no *banzai*s sounded. The Taft party was staying at the American consul's quarters on the island of Shaneen, separated by water from the main part of Canton.[343] Shaneen, owned three-fifths by Britain and two-fifths by France, was home to numerous foreign diplomatic and commercial establishments. Its massive Greco-Roman style buildings might have given the Americans the illusion that they were in London, Paris, or Geneva.

In China, the Americans couldn't count on the same welcoming warmth that had been shown to them in Japan and the Philippines. In the nineteenth century, foreigners (British, French, German, Portuguese, and others) had negotiated with Chinese officials for rights to their natural resources, railroads, and infrastructure. Corruption among Chinese government officials meant that monies paid by special interests for the concessions never benefited the general populace. Strong anti-foreigner sentiment seethed until finally, with the Boxer Rebellion, foreign enclaves in China were under attack. Although the Boxer Rebellion had been quelled, the animus toward outsiders had not dissipated.[344] At roughly the same time, many Chinese immigrants who'd toiled in the U.S. on the construction of the cross-continental railroad originally hailed from Canton and the surrounding province, and they suffered severe abuse from Americans. Then, in 1902, the U.S. Congress made the Chinese Exclusion Act permanent, in effect hanging out a "No Chinese Wanted Here" sign by forbidding Chinese laborers from immigrating to the U.S.[345] Chinese people already in the U.S. were further shunned and often subjected to great violence.[346] At the same time, U.S. diplomats were pressuring the Chinese for an "open door" policy so that Americans could sell their goods in China. Anger that was simmering now came to a rolling boil. The Cantonese feverishly promoted a boycott of U.S. goods. Newspapers headlined the boycott, turned down ads for U.S. goods, and printed the texts of incendiary speeches railing against the U.S. On the streets and in stores, posters screamed, "Do not use American goods!" and "Boycott American goods!"[347]

Taft felt they were safe on the island of Shaneen, but Consul Lay and U.S. military officers had warned him that going into Canton proper could be dangerous. He decreed to the women in the party: "You are absolutely not to go into Canton proper."[348] But Taft himself had an engagement to speak at a luncheon at the Manchu Club on Canton's mainland. Well-guarded, he made his way to the luncheon to find that his host, the viceroy of Guangdong, had sent word that he was ill and would not be there. Some claimed that this was a Cantonese snub to the Americans.

The Cantonese boycott was hurting the U.S. economy. Standard Oil's sales were down fifty percent, American flour sales were off, and sales of American-made cigarettes were drastically reduced after the Chinese began to produce their own brands in response to the boycott.[349] In his speech to the Manchu Club, Taft protested that the boycott was unfair, and that the U.S. would treat immigrants fairly. Few minds were changed.[350]

In the month before the group's arrival, handbills emblazoned with Alice Roosevelt's picture appeared on the streets of Canton. The poster showed Alice in a sedan chair carried by four turtles. Her hosts told her that being borne by turtles was a crude reflection on her ancestry. (Others said the posters were meant to discourage laborers from carrying the Americans, because the turtles stood for henpecked husbands and that's what a coolie who carried Alice would be.) Alice merely laughed at the depiction, but when American authorities complained of the insult, Cantonese authorities assured them that the culprit would be found and executed. "[When I was] told that the authors of the pamphlet would be executed . . . I had to intercede for them, to ask for mercy which I believe was granted," she wrote later.[351]

Despite these tensions, Alice wanted to see Canton, one of the world's largest cities with its enormous trading port. She found the captain of an American gunboat who agreed to take her by water, but he said she had to agree not to go ashore in the city itself. Taft agreed with the plan, as long as she followed the captain's orders not to enter the city. Accordingly, Alice saw Canton as much as she'd seen San Francisco's Chinatown: she could say she'd seen Canton, but she didn't see much of it.[352]

The party left Canton without incident and moved eighty miles down the Pearl River to Hong Kong, where Taft and Alice paid a visit to the British governor, Sir Mathew Nathan, at Government House. He entertained them at dinner where they enjoyed a magnificent view of Victoria Peak across Hong Kong's spectacular harbor, dotted with vessels of all sizes, from one-man skiffs to sailing junks to ocean-going steamships.[353]

Their time in Hong Kong was brief, but they managed to attend a ball at the Hong Kong Club and enjoy a day at the races. The riders were mounted on diminutive ponies rather than on the super-sized horses of American tracks. When one of the racers invited Alice to be a passenger in a racing rickshaw, she accepted and relished the excitement.[354]

But changes were coming.

William Howard Taft and most of the congressmen and their wives were preparing to leave for the States. Taft could leave knowing he'd accomplished his assignments: he'd determined that Japanese territorial intentions in the Far East were focused (currently, at least) on Korea and not on the Philippines; he'd been able to reassure the people of the Philippines of continued U.S. interest and support even though he could not advance the cause of immediate independence; he'd listened (and found himself sympathetic) to pleas for relief from the tariff on sugar; and he'd done the best he could with Alice.

Taft may well have been relieved to shed his responsibility for Alice. He'd confided in letters to his wife that he was uneasy about her relationship with Nick Longworth. The congressman had not impressed the secretary with his sincerity, and Taft felt that Nick's influence on Alice was not for the best. Alice was smitten with this sophisticated man who was almost twice her age, while Taft described Alice as being, in some ways, "younger than her years."[355]

The relationship between Alice and Nick was still fraught with clashes. Alice was unsure of herself and unsure of Nick. She trod an uncertain path, balancing between spending her time with Nick and spending time performing her official duties.

Secretary Taft and much of the congressional contingent said their farewells and made ready to sail for home on one of the Pacific Mail ships. Alice (the "American Princess" as she was coming to be called), along with Senator and Mrs. Newlands, Bourke Cockran, Amy McMillan, Mabel Boardman, Nicholas Longworth, Lafayette Young, and General and Mrs. Corbin, would continue north through the Yellow Sea to land near Tsientsin.[356] From there they'd go the short distance to Peking by train.

Alice, however, still needed to spread her charm on one more mission for her father: the call on Cixi, China's formidable empress dowager.

Another adventure lay ahead.

4

Tokyo: Frustrated Protesters

Cal McKnight was in a jinrickshaw in the street, in front of the home minister's residence next door to his hotel. Too late, he realized that the furious, stick-wielding, stone-throwing mob was charging toward him, his rickshaw, and his rickshaw driver. The rioters spurted like water from a firehose out of the gates of the home minister's property and into the street, pursued by mounted policemen who flailed at the erupting bodies with the scabbards of their swords. The immediate goal of the police was to prevent the mob from succeeding in its announced intention of setting fire to the minister's house. Judging from the eruption of bodies from the grounds, the police were enjoying some success.

McKnight's rickshaw was smack in the path of the irate, fast-moving protesters, and when they tried to get past, the rickshaw gave a shimmy, and suddenly McKnight, the driver, and the rickshaw were lying in the street in the midst of the stampeding crowd.

Moments earlier, McKnight had been on his way back to the hotel from the American legation when he spotted a disturbance on the street ahead. Thousands of agitated young men were milling about in the street between Hibiya Park and the grounds of the hotel. Instantly, McKnight recalled that this (September 5) was the day he'd seen on the posters urging those opposed to the peace treaty to gather in the park.

Thousands of people had answered the call for the meeting, and by this time they had managed to force their way onto the grounds of the residence of the home minister, across from the park and adjacent to McKnight's hotel.

The rickshaw driver had progressed with difficulty through the press of people until McKnight finally asked him to stop. Why were the protesters not in the park? He found someone who spoke English and asked him what happened. It seems that when the crowd began to gather, they found that the police had arrived ahead of them and had barricaded the park entrances.

McKnight had his driver draw closer. While he watched, more police arrived on horseback, charged, and fought their way onto the minister's grounds, thrashing about them with their clubs as they went. Sounds of turmoil flowed over the walls.

A few years earlier, the protest would have drawn only those people who could come on foot or by rickshaw. But with the recent completion of the Tokyo electric railway system, many more people were able to reach the center of the city. The crowd of protesters continued to grow, and their anger escalated to rage when they realized that the police were not going to allow them into the park. Their purpose in gathering had been to peacefully draw up resolutions to present to government authorities, demanding that the treaty not be ratified.

Their frustration soon found an outlet.[357]

Hibiya Park had been open only since 1903, but it had previously been the site of the residences of feudal lords and later a military parade ground. A unique feature left over from one of its previous incarnations was a water-filled moat partly surrounding the landscaped grounds.[358]

The mob continued to grow and to thrust its weight at the park gates. Finally, it reached critical mass. With a rush, the knot of human beings pushed toward the barricades and tore them down. They dealt with the policemen with a simple solution: they threw them into the moat. With the park gates forced open and the policemen immobilized, the protesters poured through.

Within a short time, they had a resolution in hand that declared their opposition to the peace treaty. What they wanted next was simple: they wanted the emperor to see the resolution. They believed he had the power to prevent ratification of the treaty. As quickly as they had entered the park, they turned to leave it. The emperor's palace was nearby, and the mob wheeled as one and headed toward the one person they believed had the power to do what they wanted. Meanwhile, other police had combined forces with the palace guard and, together, the two units prevented the mob from entering the palace grounds or getting anywhere near the emperor himself.

Frustration throbbed though the crowd. Where next? The mob was now a mobile unit, and like a river in flood, the protesters flowed through the streets. They stopped at the office of the Hochi newspaper, which was regarded as the voice of the government. The doors were barred.

Foiled once again, the mob's mood grew ugly. Within minutes, they had forced their way into the newspaper's offices and demolished everything they could lay their hands on.

Then they decided that the police were the cause of their frustration. The police, they knew, were under the control of the home minister. The grounds of the home minister's residence adjoined those of the Imperial Hotel, and it was on the street fronting both places that McKnight had now encountered the protesters.

His eyes were trying to take in the astonishing sight of thousands and thousands of young people heaving stones at the policemen who were, as far as he could tell, doing their best to guard the entrance to the grounds of the home minister's residence. Surrounding the property was a stone wall about ten feet high, broken only by two gates: one on the same street as the hotel and the other around the corner.

"The first attack was at the main gate," McKnight wrote in his journal later that day. "One small crowd with drawn swords charged in through the police line and reached the main house, but were finally driven out after two had been killed and several wounded. Once police reinforcements arrived, the officers fought their way through the mob, receiving as they did volleys of stones and clubs. When they got inside the grounds, they reformed and made a charge out at the crowd, beating them unmercifully . . ."

McKnight lingered in the street, waiting to learn the outcome. As the police continued their assault, a mass of protesters erupted through the gate, trying to get out of range of the flailing scabbards. It was then that the force of the mob landed McKnight sprawled in the street. Fortunately unhurt, he and the driver managed to get up, right the rickshaw, disentangle themselves from the crowd, and retreat safely to the Imperial Hotel next door.[359]

"Later in the afternoon the attack was on in earnest," his journal entry continued. "After a number of hand-to-hand fights with the police, in each of which the police were worsted and driven behind the walls of the compound, the crowd set fire to the lodge houses and outbuildings and managed to destroy them. Further reinforcements prevented the destruction of the main house."

To his wife, McKnight wrote that intense anti-American feeling had sprung up from the belief that Roosevelt had influenced the Japanese government to agree to unacceptable treaty terms.

"This feeling has been growing all day," he continued, and added that he believed it was responsible for what happened later that day to Dr. Lyle and himself.

That afternoon, the area in front of the hotel seethed with protesters still seeking a target for their wrath. Baron Sone, the minister of finance, had invited the Harriman party to dinner, and in spite of the violence in the streets, the dinner had not been cancelled. McKnight and Dr. Lyle emerged from the hotel on their way to the minister's home. Each hailed a rickshaw and urged his driver to take a route around the agitated crowd. The drivers insisted that the only route was straight through the horde of people. They set off.

The two Americans, in their black and white dinner clothes, stood out like clipper ships in that sea of humanity. When they reached the edge of the crowd, protesters began to shout at them in Chinese, but both men understood well enough. Their drivers wheeled around and retreated amidst an assault of rocks.

McKnight escaped untouched, but the doctor was hit in the back of the head by a rock and across the shoulders by an umbrella.

Once clear of the crowd, they stopped to assess the damage and found that the doctor's injuries were not serious. The rickshaws were dented but still functioned. The men continued on to Baron Sone's, where the guests greeted them with much concern. Dr. Lyle and McKnight made light of the incident and, in a show of bravado, assured them, "We wouldn't have missed it for the world!"[360]

The dinner was impressive, but McKnight could not help noticing that before it was served, Baron Sone and another cabinet minister, Count Chindu, were summoned out of the room. They remained away for some time, then rejoined the guests for the remainder of the evening.

Following the meal, when the ladies had gathered in another room and the men were having cigars and coffee, their hosts gathered on the far side of the room and whispered among themselves. McKnight had the feeling that something unusual was going on.

The evening passed pleasantly enough. Only when the guests were preparing to say goodnight did their hosts tell them the news: the mob was amassed between the party and the Imperial Hotel, attempting to burn down Count Chindu's home. In recalling events later, McKnight marveled at Count Chindu's grace and self-control in remaining with the guests while his home was under attack.[361]

A suspenseful hour passed at Baron Sone's as they received reports of conditions in the streets. Finally, a troop of cavalry arrived to escort the group to safety, the guests said farewell to their hosts, and the cavalry led the Americans toward the U.S. legation.

Meanwhile, the government had decided to call in the military to contain the crowds. Soldiers now patrolled the streets, herding a crowd that ebbed and flowed. At one point, a segment of the enraged mob surrounded the Americans and yelled insults at their military escorts, but the soldiers pushed on, all the way to the legation grounds.[362]

Two companies of soldiers arrived to guard the legation and informed the group that they couldn't ensure anyone's safety if they left the compound. Instead of spending the night at the Imperial Hotel, Dr. Lyle and McKnight would have to stay at the compound for the night.[363]

5

Taku Bar: Surreal Afternoon

Alice and her friends were aboard *Logan,* afloat on the mud-tinged waters of the Yellow Sea. From the decks of their transport, they could see eight warships. Fortunately, all eight ships belonged to the U.S. Navy. All were anchored eleven miles from shore outside Taku Bar, near Tsientsin, the port for Peking.

Because they'd made good time steaming north from Shanghai, they were outside Taku Bar twenty-four hours before they were expected. The local U.S. consul was to escort them ashore, but he had not yet appeared.

Entertainment was scarce, and Alice had time to ponder the fact that she was about to embark on a diplomatic mission without the comforting presence of Secretary Taft. She was entering a country where, only five years earlier, the Boxers—motivated by anti-foreigner sentiment that, reportedly, still simmered—had laid siege to the diplomatic compounds of Tsientsin and Peking, trapping foreign diplomats behind their walls for months.

Now at Taku Bar, there was little to do but much to see, so long as you liked warships. The battleships USS *Ohio III*, USS *Oregon,* and USS *Wisconsin* were supported by the cruiser *Baltimore* and five destroyers: *Bainbridge, Barry, Chauncey, Dale,* and *Decatur.*[364] The message was clear: "The daughter of the U.S. president will remain safe in your country, or there will be consequences."

The U.S. Navy was there for protection, and its personnel offered hospitality as well. When the officers of *Wisconsin* issued an invitation to a reception, everyone in the party accepted.

The ship's officers, in their crisp white uniforms, welcomed their guests, onto a deck that began to look like the verandah of a Norfolk officers' club. Music rippled through the soft September air, and impromptu dancing soon began. Alice, Amy, Mabel, and other women of the party were caught up in the arms of U.S. Navy officers who were taking full advantage of the unexpected availability of female dance partners.

The afternoon was unique, and the experience surreal. Who among them would have believed they'd be tripping the light fantastic aboard a battleship on a humid September afternoon, afloat on the mud-tinged waters of the Gulf of Chihli, in the Yellow Sea, off the coast of China?

At midnight, the U.S. consul at Tsientsin, W.W. Ragsdale, finally reached *Logan*. The next day, Alice and her friends once more fit themselves into small boats for the trip to shore.

With Consul Ragsdale, they boarded the special train that awaited them and settled into comfortable upholstered chairs in one of the parlor cars.

When the train stopped in Tsientsin to let Consul Ragsdale off, the travelers were astonished to see the platform mobbed with people who'd come to have a look at the "American princess." At the next stop, Chinese musicians blasted forth with "The Battle Hymn of the Republic" and "Yankee Doodle Dandy." Because the travelers knew that relations between China and the U.S. were far from cordial, they were astonished at the warm welcome.[365]

The train continued on through ninety miles of prairie, a patchwork of millet fields and pig farms. They finally arrived in Peking, and a new part of Alice's mission for her father began. He'd sent her on this trip with the hope that the Chinese empress dowager would be flattered to receive a visit from the daughter of the American president. He hoped that relations between the two countries would thus be improved. Before she'd left Washington, Alice had suffered anxiety about this part of the trip—she was about to appear before Cixi, China's empress dowager, the absolute ruler of one-third of the world's people and arguably the most powerful woman in the world.

6

Peking: Imperial Welcome

Alice was in a panic. It was the wine, she knew—rose wine, delicious and silky to the tongue—but much stronger than she was accustomed to. The time had long passed when she could do anything about it, and she knew that she was well on her way to being tipsy. Was she about to disgrace herself, her father, and her country? Faces blurred and she heard herself, as though at a distance, enunciating with excruciating care.

She was seated at dinner with her friends in Prince Ching's palace at the summer residence of Cixi, the empress dowager. The day had been a long one: sightseeing in the Forbidden City; a journey from the city to the beautiful grounds of the summer palace; and then a huge dinner of European dishes served with champagne and Chinese dishes served with the treacherous rose wine. Alice found the wine delicious, like a sake or smooth liqueur.[366] Too delicious, perhaps.

When they'd arrived in Peking two days before, the party was greeted by William W. Rockhill, the U.S. Minister to China, in company with a delegation of Chinese court officials, most of whom had been educated at Harvard or Oxford. Rockhill had been identified with China for so long that he was known as an "old China hand," meaning he was a Westerner with long-term experience in China. Alice described him as being pale and tall and thought that if he wore Chinese clothes, let his moustache grow, and pulled it down at the corners, he could have passed as a Chinese sage.

Using his position as U.S. minister to approach the Chinese powers-that-be, Rockhill was able to arrange for Alice and her friends to enjoy the privilege of entering the Forbidden City, often pictured but rarely visited by Westerners. They saw the expected pagoda roofs and surfaces adorned with carvings of writhing dragons, but what Alice (who had been reading Marco Polo's twelfth century *Travels*) did not expect to see was that the road between the Temple of Heaven and Peking still fit Marco Polo's description: ". . . the same shifting, hurrying crowd, the same street sounds, the same beggars, the same smells."

Inside the heavy stone walls of Peking's diplomatic compound, Alice stayed with the Rockhills at the American legation. Empress Cixi would receive them at her summer residence some distance from the city, and had invited Alice, Mabel Boardman, and Mrs. Newlands to spend the night there before their audience. To travel the sixteen miles from Peking, Alice and the Rockhills rode in a tired-looking one-horse carriage, surrounded by a cloud of dust created by their escort, a troop of Chinese soldiers wearing old straw hats, clad in faded blue uniforms, and riding run-down horses decked in run-down trappings.[367]

When they had maneuvered their way through gates that pierced a series of coral-colored walls, they found their way to Prince Ching's palace. The palace consisted of a series of connected rooms situated in a square with an open courtyard in the center. Indoors and out, exuberant, multi-colored decorations livened every surface.[368] Surfaces that were not ornately decorated were painted in distinctive, fiery Chinese red.

Alice had settled into her suite of rooms, and when dinner was announced, she and her friends had gathered in the courtyard. The wine served with the meal was the cause of her present problem. If not completely inebriated, she was at the very least having difficulty with her equilibrium. Because she'd already planned an early night in view of the next morning's early audience, she rose and took aim at the door to her suite. There it stood, at the other end of the courtyard, a door she needed to reach by walking the length of the room with her dignity intact. It would be unforgiveable to do otherwise. She steeled herself, said a distinct, "Goodnight, Mabel," and another, "Goodnight, Mrs. Newlands," and with intense concentration, walked an arrow-straight path to the door.[369]

Hoping she hadn't disgraced herself, Alice threw herself across the bed and immediately fell asleep, unmindful of the rock-hard pillow, only to wake a few hours later still in her evening clothes. She scrambled into her nightgown with the knowledge that her maid Anna, who would come in to wake her, would have been absolutely horrified if she found Alice fully clothed and in a stupor. "She was one of those sour, frightfully superior beings," Alice recalled later, "and I think she must have hated the whole trip."

At eight the next morning, Alice and the others in the party (including those who had just arrived that morning from Peking) were ready for the audience with the empress. Everyone was provided with scented soap, perfume, and a basin—but no water—to make themselves pristine for the ceremony, while officials, amahs, and eunuchs hovered solicitously. Finally, the travelers were escorted to the audience hall.[370]

The majority of the ten women in the party wore the white outfits they'd brought for the heat of the Philippines. Because the women had learned only a short time before that, for the Chinese as well as the Japanese, white was the color for funerals, they added colorful scarves to counteract the funereal effect. Meanwhile, Alice appeared in a pink dress with a black hat, trying only to counteract the effects of last night's wine.

Ten women and thirty men were to be presented, including Admiral Train and his captains (who had met them at Taku Bar), and General Corbin, flanked by his aides. All were bedecked with their medals and ribbons to lend the party what Mabel Boardman described as "a brilliant and official air."[371]

The audience-seekers waited until, finally, the signal came. Minister Rockhill and the men were summoned for their audience, which was brief. Then, the women gathered with Mrs. Rockhill and crossed the court to the single-story building. Alice, aware that this audience was why she had come halfway around the world, aware that the world was watching, and aware that it might determine whether she would stand or fall in her father's eyes, was also aware that she was still a bit unsteady from last night's over-indulgence.

Skirts held high, the ladies climbed the steps, crossed the porch, entered through the double doors, and found themselves in the throne room in the presence of the legendary Empress Cixi herself.

As a young woman, Cixi had been one of the emperor's concubines and had borne him a son. After the emperor's death, the infant son succeeded to the throne as Emperor Tongzhi, and Cixi maneuvered to become regent as well as empress dowager. When the young Emperor Tongzhi died, Cixi managed to have her sister's three-year-old son crowned Emperor Ghantzu, and herself once more declared regent.[372] She somehow managed all this in China when no woman—not even the empress dowager—was allowed in the main buildings of the Forbidden City.[373]

As regent, Cixi had enemies. She wielded absolute power and used it to do away with those she thought were plotting against her.[374] Thus, her reputation was one of ruthlessness. On the other hand, she loved her country passionately. Some of her councilors wanted China to remain isolated from the rest of the world, but Cixi disagreed, believing it was time to adopt more modern ways. Under Cixi's rule, railroads, electricity, the telegraph, telephones, medicine, expanded diplomacy, and the beginning of education for women had come to China.[375]

Cixi had several close friends who were American women, and now she was about to meet dozens more Americans, including the "American princess."[376]

With Mrs. Rockhill to introduce her, Alice made her way toward the empress, who was seated on a carved teakwood throne, elevated on a dais. To Alice, it seemed that she was crossing a great expanse as she steered her slightly unsteady self toward the throne, making the obligatory three curtsies as she went forward.[377]

As she drew closer, Alice could see the upright, uncompromising posture of the petite, seventy-year-old empress.[378] Gold-sheathed fingernails tipped the hand that rested on the arm of the raised throne. She wore a loose blue coat edged with a rich band of silk embroidery with an underskirt of yellow (blue and yellow were the Chinese colors for royalty). Her face was unpainted, an acknowledgement of her widowed state, and her sleek, dark hair was adorned with a headdress in the high Manchu style, the hair formed into a sort of bow from which hung three strands of baroque pearls. Emerging from the center of the headdress were carved pieces of deep green jade.[379] One could wonder: if the hairdo were arranged the night before, did she sleep sitting up?

Many years later, Alice recalled that the empress looked younger than her years and exuded character and power. Her face was distinguished by piercing black eyes and a thin mouth turned up at one end and drooped at the other, appearing rather cruel, Alice thought. Her face was memorable, and her charm obvious.

After Mrs. Rockhill presented Alice, the empress picked up a small book from which she read a greeting translated by Wu Tin Fang, former Chinese minister in Washington. In a less formal mode, the empress remarked that Alice had come such a long way from her country. "I hope you are not suffering from homesickness," she said.

"I have been received with such kindness everywhere that it has not been possible to be homesick," Alice replied quickly.[380]

Her part in the audience now over, Alice now had to get herself down the steps, off the platform, and across the room without turning her back on the empress, and without tripping and tumbling in an ignominious heap. She was still not feeling steady on her feet. Moving cautiously, she stepped backward, feeling her way to the edge of the dais. With an acrobat's focus, she stepped gingerly down and backed gracefully off to the sidelines, where she stood while the empress came down off the platform to greet the other women.

Alice had time to look around while the others were introduced. She saw that Emperor Guangtzu was there, huddled on the lowest step of the dais. But his presence was barely acknowledged. "His mouth [was] a little open, his eyes dull and wandering, no expression in his face," she noted, adding that the Americans were not presented to him.[381] Mabel Boardman observed that the emperor looked ten years younger than his thirty-four years.

Two of the emperor's wives and an elderly Chinese princess entertained the women at lunch. The royal women spoke no English, and the Americans spoke no Chinese dialect, but they were not deterred from conversation. Their interpreter was Mrs. Williams, wife of the legation's interpreter. Sorting out the conversations for fifteen women must have been a challenge to her skills.

Following the luncheon, Empress Cixi joined them in the gardens, and through an interpreter, exchanged pleasantries with each of her visitors. She presented each with a gift of heavy gold jewelry and said she hoped that they'd all had a pleasant night's stay. Those who'd spent the night in Prince Ching's palace remembered the generous tea, dinner, and breakfast they'd been served and forbore mentioning the rock-like pillows and the lack of water. The empress suddenly decided that the emperor should take a larger part in the festivities and proceeded to present each of the women to him. While Alice found the emperor somewhat vacant, Mabel Boardman saw him as a man with physical challenges, a man who did not speak, and who seemed to avoid any conflict with the empress dowager. Mabel thought his world-weary smile indicated amusement with what he saw. Mr. Wu had been interpreting all the while when the empress turned suddenly from her guests and spoke harshly to him. Mr. Wu dropped down and touched his forehead to the ground. He continued to interpret from this humiliating position and no explanation was ever given.[382]

"It was a curious experience to see the same man who enjoyed making blandly insolent remarks at dinner parties in Washington and invidious comments on America in press interviews, kowtowing at someone's feet," Alice remarked. What the Americans did not realize was that Cixi's subjects were required to prostrate themselves before her, a rule she never relaxed. The ambassador had become used to being upright in the presence of Westerners, and she reminded him that in China he still needed to lower himself before her.[383]

After the empress withdrew, the Americans continued their tour of the garden. Most were on foot, but Alice was borne in an imperial yellow chair high on the shoulders of eight bearers. She enjoyed the experience hugely. "There are few things lovelier than the sweep of a Chinese roof, the eaves painted in brilliant greens, blues, and vermilions, and often the eaves and roof ridge decorated with grotesque figures of dragons, phoenixes, and lion dogs." It was truly magical for Alice—". . . fantastic, incredible, Cathay of the old tales," she said.

As the final segment of their visit to the summer palace, they sat in the replica of a Chinese "junk" (a ship) built at the edge of a lake. As they ate the authentic Chinese meal that followed, Alice discovered that she particularly liked the ancient eggs (preserved eggs with a greenish yolk and gelatinous white). When it was time to return to Peking, the travelers boarded small boats and floated down the canal that connected the palace grounds with Peking, gracefully ending a day that none of them would ever forget.

Back at the legation, Alice discovered that the empress was not finished with her gift giving. The next day, two officials appeared and presented Alice with a little black Pekinese dog—the empress had her own kennel—which Alice quickly named Manchu. She carried him back to Washington and cared for him for many years. Later the same day, a troop of cavalry arrived escorting an imperial yellow chair occupied only by a box wrapped in imperial yellow brocade. Inside the box was a picture, in a standard gilt frame, of Empress Cixi herself.

China had charmed Alice Roosevelt. As her father's representative, she did her duty and spent much of her time socializing with representatives of various governments. Their stay was too brief, she complained, to see the Ming tombs and the Great Wall. She promised herself that she would return every two years.[384] She never did.

ᔓ

While Alice had been exploring Peking, William Howard Taft was on board SS *Siberia*, which had made its way as far as Kobe, Japan on its way to San Francisco. Disturbed by the change in Japanese attitudes toward the U.S., he cabled Minister Rockhill in Peking: "Conditions in Japan and especially in large cities make it unwise for Miss Roosevelt to spend any considerable time in Japan in the near future. Advise that she change her plans so as to spend her time in China, taking *Siberia* at Shanghai. Confer with her, Mrs. Newlands, and party and answer me care consulate in Yokohama."[385]

7
Tokyo: Flaming Spider

The situation was worrisome. McKnight wrote to May, "If the troops remain loyal to the government, of which there is grave doubt, there will be no danger to the foreign population. But if they side with the rioters who seem to have the sympathy of the whole population, then there will be the greatest danger to all foreigners, especially Americans."[386]

Confined to the legation, McKnight and the others were reminded uneasily of the Boxer Rebellion in China, five short years before when Westerners had been trapped under siege in Peking's diplomatic compound for almost two months.

The present situation in Tokyo was unnervingly similar. The Tokyo protesters had a sense of grievance against the Americans in their midst because of President Roosevelt's brokering of the detested peace treaty. For the legation's guests, the possibility of violent attacks provided a frightening vision.

However, the Boxers had enjoyed support in China—mostly secret—from the government, and certainly had access to armaments.[387] In Japan, the protesters were antagonistic to the police, seeing them as tools of an administration about to ratify an unfair peace treaty. On the other hand, the protesters were respectful of the army as victors in battle and upholders of the national honor. And the Japanese protesters did not have access to arms.

The nights of September 5 and September 6 saw the arrival of masses of Japanese army troops, who succeeded in quieting disturbances in the neighborhood of the American legation. By morning, the streets were calm enough that McKnight and Dr. Lyle were able to return to the Imperial Hotel.

The day passed in relative quiet, but in the afternoon, McKnight became aware of men gathering once more in the streets outside the minister's home next door, now under military guard.

All policemen had been removed from duty and the maintenance of order was now completely in the hands of the military. "The mob didn't seem as vicious toward the soldiers and the soldiers seemed to be more in sympathy with the crowd," McKnight observed.

The crowd was growing. Early in the evening, the streets in the vicinity of the Imperial Hotel were crowded with men heading for the home minister's residence, once again the focus of the protesters. By seven in the evening, McKnight judged that the crowd was perhaps fifty-thousand strong, and by eight o'clock, had nearly doubled in size.

The Imperial Hotel was in the center of the disturbed area. Anxiety among the spectators at the hotel intensified when they heard about a message delivered to the nearby electric company from the protesters: "You are to shut down operations at nine this evening." If the company's managers did not comply, the protesters threatened to destroy the electric plant.

At the same time, a current of rumors was running through the hotel that the mob's next move would be an attack on the foreign legations. The American legation would be a special target. Until then, McKnight had been inclined to regard the events of the past two days as interesting and exciting, but now the situation was becoming serious. He telephoned the U.S. legation and spoke with Minister Griscom.

"I've just heard that the electric company will be attacked if they don't shut down operations at nine tonight," McKnight reported. When he'd verified McKnight's report by calling the electric company himself, Griscom notified the government authorities. Shortly, more troops arrived to guard the plant and to force the company to keep the electricity on.

Meanwhile, a heavy military guard was successfully keeping the mob from reaching the home minister's house next door. Diverted from its targets, the crowd found a new outlet for its energies: trolley cars. Trolley tracks bordered the spacious streets in this part of Tokyo, and the crowd was able to lay its hands on eight or ten trolley cars in the vicinity of the hotel. They set each trolley car ablaze. Then, from opposite directions, they'd send two blazing cars toward each other to meet with a resounding crash—totally destroying each other as if they'd agreed on a mutual suicide pact.

Inside the hotel, the guests were growing increasingly uneasy, especially when it was learned that the hotel was sheltering the home minister and his family. The guests worried that if the mob were to learn of the home minister's whereabouts, the hotel would become a focal point for the crowd's fury.

At about eleven that night, large bodies of troops poured into the blocks around the hotel. After repeated charges from different directions, they succeeded in fracturing the crowd into smaller groups. Each group moved off in a different direction.

McKnight had gone to the roof of the hotel to view the action. From there, he could watch as different groups were detached from the main body of protesters and forced away from the center of the disturbance. Having found fire a gratifying means of expressing their anger, members of each group used their new tool unsparingly as they proceeded along their way. Each time they came upon a police kiosk, they torched it; any previously untouched trolley car was set alight; churches and homes were targets as well. The progress of the different bands could be followed by their trails of fire. In less than an hour, Tokyo looked like a giant flaming spider.

The fires burned for much of the night, but by morning, quiet had descended upon the city. In the course of the disturbance, the mob had torched trolley cars, homes, more than one hundred police stations and kiosks, and Christian churches of various denominations.[388]

More troops were arriving as fast as the railroads could carry them. On the morning of September 7, the government placed Tokyo under martial law.[389] The police withdrew completely from the city's streets and were replaced by patrols of soldiers with orders to shoot anyone who refused to follow their orders. All government buildings, homes of officials, and foreign legations were placed under a strong guard of troops. R. P. Schwerin, head of the Pacific Mail Steamship Line, was trying to access the U.S. legation when the crowd barred his way. Before he could get away, his rickshaw drivers were attacked, but Schwerin was unhurt.[390]

"Our Japanese friends called off all dinners and parties because of the danger," McKnight wrote to May, "and we concluded it would be wise to seek quieter quarters."

ꟹ

Harriman wanted to come to some understanding with Japanese officials about the future of the Manchurian railroads and his part in that future. Thanks to Lloyd Griscom, he'd met most of those who would make the decisions. He just needed time with them to present his case.[391] At the moment, Japanese officialdom was focused on stabilizing the riotous segments of the populace. He'd come up against a totally unpredictable obstacle to his plans.

Harriman and his family were still lodged at the American legation. With the sense that current circumstances made their presence too great a responsibility for his hosts, Harriman decided that they would leave Tokyo—temporarily, at least.[392]

When it would be safe to return, he didn't know.

8

Nikko and Kyoto: Tourists and Shoppers

Cal McKnight was torn. Should he, or shouldn't he? Would May like it, or would she think him foolish? He was looking at an antelope rug, a bargain at the Japanese equivalent of six dollars. It was not the sort of thing most of their family and friends would have on their floors, and it would certainly be a conversation piece.

McKnight had wandered into one of Nikko's appealing shops. The area's tranquil mountains and cooler air were proving a welcome contrast to Tokyo's tumultuous streets and overcharged atmosphere. The residents of this summer resort town seemed largely unaware of the unrest in the capital. Temporarily at least, the government had effectively muffled reports of the riots and had temporarily forbidden three newspapers to publish anything about the clashes. On the other hand, the municipal government of Tokyo had sided with the protesters and passed a resolution saying the treaty should be abrogated.[393]

Thanks to the hoorah over the Portsmouth treaty terms, Harriman couldn't continue to focus on persuading the Japanese government to let him share control over the formerly Russian-held railways in Manchuria. This would not be the only time that the treaty's stipulations would throw him off course, although next time, they would affect him more directly. As it was, Harriman made the decision to journey with his family to Nikko, north of Tokyo.

Courtesy of the Nippon Railway, the Harrimans, McKnight, and the rest of the party traveled by special train. If Harriman had any questions to do with railway operations, the line's managing director, its passenger superintendent, and its maintenance superintendent were all available aboard the train.[394]

As a tourist destination, Nikko had everything: agreeable climate; woods; mountain views. A well-known Japanese saying warns, "Don't use the word 'magnificent' without seeing Nikko." It had extinct volcanoes, waterfalls, and hot springs. An elaborate shrine was built in Nikko as a mausoleum for Tokugawa Ieyasu, a shogun of the military government that had formerly ruled Japan for hundreds of years.

And as if all those attractions weren't enough, Nikko had become a sacred place for two religions. The Buddhist priest Shodo Shonin had established a hermitage there, and Nikko was now the site of an institution for the training of Buddhist monks. Nikko was also a center of Shinto, the indigenous religion of Japan. The earliest Japanese people believed that humans had a special relationship with mountains and trees. Because of their perception of several of the nearby mountains as sacred, Nikko became a center of Shinto religious practice. Shrines were built there and dedicated to the mountains.

In the mid-nineteenth century, at the time of the emperor's restoration and the beginning of modernization, Zenichiro Kanaya was a member of the orchestra in the Toshogu Shrine. Looking about, Kanaya realized that Englishmen, Germans, and other Westerners were coming to Japan to consult with the government on military and educational matters. Because Japan had been closed to foreigners for centuries, these visitors were anxious to see the country. Nikko, with its trove of temples, inspiring scenery, and pleasant summer temperatures, was a magnet for foreigners. Kanaya decided to build a hotel with views of the mountains that would cater to Western visitors, and in 1873, he opened the first building.[395] That summer of 1905, the Kanaya Hotel hosted the Harriman entourage.

Still looking at the antelope rug, McKnight finally decided in its favor, and a few days later, he would be faced with further temptations in Japan's former capital, Kyoto. But although Nikko's shops were alluring, as were the Buddhist temples and Shinto shrines, McKnight felt the finest attractions were the trees and the mountains themselves. When the opportunity came to join a group headed for Lake Minoshu, he seized it.

The lake was ten miles away, and the sightseers rode horseback through country that, for McKnight, brought back memories of Virginia's mountains, where he'd ridden horseback and cruised timber for the family lumber business. Instead of oak and hickory, here was Cryptomeria, the lush blue-green Japanese cedar, fifty to sixty feet tall.[396] At one time, an avenue of these stately trees had extended all the way from Tokyo to Nikko. By the turn of the twentieth century, the avenue had been shortened to only half its length.

The four days spent in the cool of the mountains were an agreeable change of pace from the constant round of dinners and receptions given them by their Tokyo hosts. By three o'clock on September 11, however, the Harrimans and their companions arrived back in Tokyo, where the sight of uniformed soldiers everywhere reminded them of the unsettling events less than a week before.[397]

First on the agenda for Harriman, his friend Robert Goelet, and R.B. Schwerin was a visit to the imperial palace, where His Imperial Majesty, the emperor of Japan, granted them an audience.[398] Actual power to rule Japan resided with the oligarchs, but the emperor was the country's respected titular head. When he had moved from Kyoto to Tokyo early in his long rule and was anxious to endear himself to his new neighbors, the story goes that the emperor began by distributing sake to the local population. He had married Ichijo Haruko, daughter of a court official. She was childless, but the emperor had fifteen children by various ladies-in-waiting. Only one son, Crown Prince Yoshihito, and four princesses—Masako, Fusako, Nobuko, and Toshiko—survived to adulthood.[399]

Another member of the imperial family, Prince Fushimi, had invited the entire party to dinner at his home that evening. The prince had visited the U.S. a few months before, where he had received celebrity treatment. Tonight's hospitality was a way of reciprocating.[400]

When Dr. Lyle and McKnight were ready to leave the hotel for the prince's residence, they found an escort of cavalry waiting for them. "It wasn't at all necessary as the best of order now prevails," McKnight wrote to his wife. "All streets are patrolled by the troops. Of course, we felt very important as we passed through the streets with our escort."

Just as McKnight and Dr. Lyle were stepping into their carriage on their way to the dinner party, word came that mail from the States had arrived at the legation. The two had traveled for almost a month without receiving any mail and were anxious to hear from their families. They were homesick.

"We wanted to go there at once in the worst way and get our letters," McKnight wrote to his wife, "but the invitation of an imperial prince is a command . . . all etiquette demands that instead of being late as is the custom at an ordinary function, one must arrive at least ten minutes ahead of the time fixed in the invitation so as to be in the reception room when the prince comes down. So much to our disgust we had to go on to the dinner and wait until it was over before we could go to the legation for the mail."

The majority of the dinner guests were members of the nobility, and they, the prince, and the American minister were attired in uniformed splendor. Gold braid gleamed and medals glittered. Hosts and guests dined on thirteen courses based on French cuisine: *filets de sole* à *la Normande*; *côtelettes de veau aux purée de marrons*; *pâté de foie-gras* à *la Diplomate*; *génoise* à *la crème*; and *pailles au parmesan*.

"The ladies present . . . were princesses and wives of nobles. Conversation was rather limited as many of them couldn't speak English and of those who could, few spoke fluently," McKnight's letter continued.[401]

One evening before they were to leave for Kyoto, Harriman, in his usual precipitous fashion with a total absence of preliminaries, said to Griscom, "There's no doubt about it. If I can secure control of the South Manchurian Railroad from Japan, I'll buy the Chinese Eastern from Russia, acquire trackage over the Trans-Siberian to the Baltic, and establish a line of steamers to the United States. Then I can connect with the American transcontinental lines and join up with the Pacific Mail and the Japanese transcontinental steamers." He added confidently, "It'll be the most marvelous transportation system in the world. We'll girdle the earth."

A startled Griscom inquired as to how Harriman would deal with the enormous challenges of coming up with huge amounts of capital, accommodating the as-yet-unknown needs of the track itself, and meeting the requirements for new rolling stock.

"The way to find out what is best to be done is to start doing something," Harriman replied. Then he leaned in and added, "You know all these Japanese [officials]. I want you to help me."

Unsettled by Harriman's request, Griscom felt he was on delicate ground. He knew that relations between Theodore Roosevelt and Harriman, once close and warm, were now distant and beyond frigid—the president's reputation as someone who was keeping trusts and monopolies under control was in direct conflict with Harriman's work in building empires. Griscom also knew his own diplomatic future depended on the president's good will. But he must have thought that if Harriman could put through his deal, American trade in Manchuria and Korea would advance by leaps and bounds. Griscom considered and finally told Harriman he'd do what he could, and then sat down and wrote a letter to the president explaining why he'd agreed to help Harriman. He also asked for permission to take leave and accompany Harriman to Manchuria. When permission was denied, Griscom turned his attention to moving the Japanese officials along toward decisions favorable to Harriman.[402]

On September 13, at seven in the evening, the Harriman party gathered at the railway station, ready to leave Tokyo once more. Their numbers were shrinking. Groton's headmaster had refused to give young Averell Harriman permission to extend his summer vacation. Accompanied by his tutor, Octavious Bates, and Hugh Neill, his father's Union Pacific secretary, Averell left the party at Nikko and took only a short tour of Kyoto, Naro, and Kamakura on the way to Yokohama. There, they would board SS *Korea*, scheduled to sail for San Francisco on September 17.[403]

Several high officials were at the station to see the larger Harriman party off. "The Japanese are the most polite people in the world and that applies to all classes from the nobles down to the coolies and rickshaw men," McKnight noted. "Of course, there were a few days in Tokyo when politeness was forgotten on the streets, but it seemed as though [our hosts] were doubly polite in attempting to eradicate any bad impressions we had received."[404]

They traveled all night in two sleeping cars, reported to be the only two first-class cars in the country, which were transported two hundred miles just to be used for their journey to Kyoto.

When the party arrived at ten the next morning, they found Kyoto to be a city embraced by a ring of mountains and home to more than a million people. The travelers settled into the Mikayo Hotel across from the old capitol, seat of the Mikados for centuries. The weather was so hot, however, that it stifled any immediate desire to set out on a sightseeing tour.[405] The group rested and hoped that a cooling breeze would roll down from the wooded mountains to dislodge the humid, smothering air.

The next day, when they finally ventured out, they were faced with dizzying choices. Gardens, for instance. A garden framed each of Kyoto's sixteen hundred Buddhist temples and Shinto shrines. Should they tour a zen garden, framed by a wall, its gravel raked into rhythmic patterns and its rocks and stones perhaps representing the cranes or tortoises that symbolized longevity? But a zen garden could only be admired from the gate, not entered. If they wished to explore, they could amble through a strolling garden, lush with vegetation: cherry trees that flowered in season; maples whose leaves would, in the next few weeks, transform themselves into scarlet clouds; and chrysanthemums poised to punctuate the landscape with exclamation points of yellow, pink, and lavender.

The shrines and temples themselves ranged from the brilliant Heian shrine, with its vermilion bulk topped by a graceful green tile pagoda roof, to the subdued half-timbered shrine of Toyotomi Hideyoshi, the warlord who'd unified Japan three hundred years before.

It was under the graceful, flowing A-line roof of the Hideyoshi shrine that Harriman encountered several men who were dressed in what looked like remnants of uniforms. They were not Japanese.

"Who are they?" he whispered to their interpreter.

"Russian prisoners of war," was the answer. They were survivors of the battle of Tsu Shima, and their number included Admiral Rozhestvensky and Admiral Nebogatov.

Harriman would not disturb the privacy of the officers but did engage a number of the enlisted men in conversation through interpreters. Most of them, he discovered, were raw recruits with little military experience. "They seemed well contented and well cared for," McKnight reported.[406] Other Kyoto temples were also temporary homes for the prisoners who were perhaps surprised to find themselves transferred from hospital quarters in Sasebo, where they'd barely survived for several months, to these elegant temples and shrines amidst beautifully groomed gardens.

Less than forty years before, when the shoguns lost power and the emperor and his court moved from Kyoto to Tokyo, Kyoto had struggled to find a new identity. The city's craftsmen had been focused on producing beautiful objects for the emperor and those who surrounded him, but suddenly that market was no more. Then, in the latter part of the nineteenth century, the rest of the world discovered an enthusiasm for things Japanese, and Kyoto took on a new persona. The city's craftspeople, who had supplied the emperor and his court with exquisitely worked treasures, were now able to satisfy the cravings of foreigners for prints, brasses, enamels, embroideries, and porcelains.

Finding themselves in a city with a reputation as a source of collectible items, the Americans shifted into serious acquisition mode. "I am told this is a good place to buy old Japanese and Chinese artwork and shall put in some time tomorrow going through the shops," McKnight wrote to May.

On his outing to the shops the next day, there was no need to deliberate about the gift he would bring home for his three-year-old daughter, Mary: a tiny kimono with a vibrant flower print on a white background, with flowing sleeves trimmed in red and finished with a red traditional "obi," or sash.

But McKnight found himself intrigued by many other items, including a unique and graceful ten-inch tall, four-sided brass vase with a six-inch detachable lizard adorning one face. He found a delicate silk wall hanging about eighteen inches square, depicting a branch of cherry blossoms embroidered in glistening silk thread.

Then there were the prints, in all sizes and shapes and subjects: garden scenes; mini landscapes of seaside villages; and scenes from Japanese theater, including a mysterious one of two gentlemen having a sword fight in a rowboat. And there was a macabre series of blue and black depictions of empty skulls.[407]

What to do?

Simple. He bought them all.

McKnight discovered later, when he took on the job of inventorying everyone's purchases to be put aboard the ship for home, that he was neither the only shopper nor the biggest purchaser.

Kyoto was warm, and the Americans moved at a slower pace than in Tokyo. Harriman was busy finishing plans for the next phase of their journey. He wanted to go to Manchuria. A first-hand look at the Manchurian Railway would let him know what there was to do in the way of reconstruction. Lloyd Griscom, remembering vividly the opposition he'd met when he attempted to get permissions for the reporters, was not encouraging. Griscom did not believe that Japanese officialdom would allow Harriman and company into what had so recently been a war zone.

To Griscom's astonishment, the officials were cooperative; but there was one snag: because the Manchurian ports had been closed during the war, there were no regularly scheduled ships available to carry them there.[408] But Harriman was in the transportation business, and to him the solution was obvious: charter a ship. The ship he engaged was *Ohio III*, a small freighter with passenger accommodations.

Captain Matsumoto of the Japanese army's general staff arrived to escort them to Manchuria.[409] It was time to go.

9
Seoul: Sad Scenes

Alice's pen moved furiously across the legation stationery: "[When] you left this morning and I asked if you felt any better about me," she began, "you said, 'no I do not,' in a tone of such frank dislike and with an expression of such active disgust that if I did not love you so much would make me never wish to see you again."[410]

Before they left the states, Alice believed that she and Nick were as good as engaged. By the time they'd worked their way to Korea and spent more than two months in each other's company, their relationship was tacking into a high wind with lots of ups and downs. They continued to quarrel frequently. They were conducting this tumultuous courtship under the eyes of Alice's chaperones and in the glare of the publicity provided by the reporters who were covering the trip. After Secretary Taft's departure for the States, Mrs. Newlands was the remaining chaperone and the reporters were fewer. Alice's big assignments were behind her, and her principal chore was simply to respond to the hospitality of the Korean emperor and of Korea's Japanese officials. She and Nick should have been enjoying a relaxing interlude together now that Alice's official duties were largely behind her, but as in the history of their relationship, things were not going smoothly between Alice and the man she'd set her heart on.

Was Nick having second thoughts about marriage? He'd been spoiled by his mother and sisters who, by the time Nick was thirty-seven, expected that he might never marry. Although he'd reportedly been engaged several times, he'd managed to remain a bachelor long after most men his age were enjoying family life. Alice was only a few years removed from girlhood, while Nick was an experienced gallant accustomed to accompanying sophisticated women older than Alice. If their expectations of each other were unrealistic, their disputes were not surprising. Still, they had almost another month in which to determine whether or not Nick would really ask Theodore Roosevelt for his daughter's hand in marriage.

The Korean government had been pleased when it was announced that Alice Roosevelt and her friends would be paying a visit. The emperor and his officials nourished the forlorn hope that her visit might nudge the U.S. to take up their cause and prevent the Japanese takeover already in progress. They resolved to put on an impressive welcome for the president's daughter and escort her with a squad of mounted Korean cavalrymen in elegant red uniforms. But as Willard Straight wrote to a friend, "Paddock [on the legation staff] stopped that because the Korean cavalry can only stick on by hanging on to the pommels of their saddles and at any function are always sure to fall off, while their ponies invariably run away. Thus, we are deprived of the special circus parade."[411]

Minister Morgan and Willard Straight, together with Korean officials, met Alice and her friends when they arrived in Chemulpo. A special train then delivered them to Seoul. From there, Alice was transported to the U.S. legation compound like royalty, in the emperor's imperial yellow sedan chair, propelled by four bearers and flanked by men carrying lanterns on long poles. The emperor's bodyguard lined the way and white-robed Koreans filled the streets.[412]

"His Majesty of all the Koreas" (as Straight termed him) granted Alice and her friends an audience at his quarters, in a sprawling compound where each building was topped by an imposing pagoda roof. Inside, they found themselves under ceilings painted like brilliant rectangular parasols, in exuberant floral patterns vibrant with reds, greens, yellows, and blues. The emperor, ensconced on a red throne, received them with the crown prince at hand.

On another day, the emperor invited them to luncheon in a European part of the palace. As Alice remembered the occasion, "We were received in an upstairs room, and then the squat emperor did not give me his arm, but took mine, and together we went in a hurried wobble down a very narrow staircase to an un-noteworthy, smallish dining room. We had Korean food, served in Korean dishes and bowls ornamented with the imperial crest. Those I used were afterward presented to me, and at a farewell audience, the emperor and crown prince each gave me his photograph."

Alice knew that Korea was coming under Japanese control and that the emperor and his son had very little imperial existence ahead of them. Although she appreciated the hospitality, after being in the commanding presence of Japan's emperor and China's empress dowager, Alice thought the tentative demeanor of the Korean emperor and prince made them seem rather pathetic. Alice observed that Korea, reluctant and helpless, was sliding into the grasp of Japan. "The whole people looked sad and dejected, all strength seemed to have been drained from them. Everywhere there were Japanese officers and troops, militant and workmanlike; a contrast to the poor abject Koreans."[413]

Socializing continued. Willard Straight accompanied the travelers to a concert by the Korean military band. But, with no understanding of Korean music, what he heard was "the weirdest and most awesome noise—shrieks and the tumming of tom-toms, the shrill voice of the flute and the rolling of a base horn."[414]

Both Japanese and Koreans labored diligently to entertain the guests with dinners and garden parties, and before their ten-day visit was up, Alice was sated with being "temporary royalty," as she put it. "How real royalty can stand it, in season and out, is hard to imagine," she mused.[415]

Willard Straight proved to be a welcome diversion.

Except for Amy McMillan, Alice's current traveling companions had all left behind the lively days of their twenties. Willard Straight, on the other hand, had yet to reach thirty. He was still producing drawings of people he encountered; he played the guitar; he wrote poetry. And he knew how to have fun. Alice was much wrapped up in Nick, and Willard Straight became a friend to both, an association that endured long past their time in Korea.

The friendship, as it turned out, would affect the course of Straight's future.

He penned some verses titled "Alice in Plunderland" and presented them to a greatly pleased Alice. The words are a light-hearted take on Straight's feeling about Korea and what was happening to it:

When Alice came to Plunderland,
The Crown Prince sought her lily hand,
The Emperor had a pipe
Dream that this was where his native land
Could shake the Japs forever and
Secure a friendship ripe
With father.

But, now there's trouble brewing, for
The Emperor doth reign no more,
The Japanese are out for wealth,
They're not in business for their health.
The Koreans wail, "What can we do?
Our clothes is picked, our watches, too.
Our country's in receivers' hands.
We've neither graft nor fees,
Since Alice came to Plunderland
We've nothing left to "squeeze."[416]

Straight was finding it painful to watch the transformation of what had been a separate country into a fiefdom of an oppressor nation. His opinion of the Japanese diminished daily as their presence became more visible and their actions more controlling. The Japanese intended to take over Korea's foreign policy, and when that happened there would be no need for U.S. or other foreign representatives to the Korean government. Straight's days in Seoul were numbered.[417]

Straight had been assigned the task of shepherding the group of visitors during their time in Seoul. He arranged one form of entertainment that the visitors found to be a pleasant respite from formal occasions: horseback riding.

They rode nearly every afternoon. Alice joked later about one pony who she said had a particular aversion to her. When Alice was sure that the groom had a good grip on the hostile horse, she would stand about ten feet back and make a face at it. In response, the pony would lay back its ears, bare its yellow teeth, and struggle, unsuccessfully, to shake off the groom and get to Alice.

One day, they rode to the imperial tombs of the Yi dynasty. Straight snapped a picture of Alice in riding boots and a divided skirt as she posed astride a funerary stone horse, a perhaps sacrilegious act from a Korean point of view. Their rides brought them back just at dusk, when they could enjoy the sight of the mountains silhouetted by light from the setting sun.[418]

When it was time to leave Korea, U.S. Consul Edward Morgan joined them for the train trip down the Korean peninsula. They departed from Seoul's wooden station on the Gyeongbu railroad, built by the Japanese using forced Korean labor and finished only ten months earlier. Morgan's attendants took over part of the baggage car and used it as a place to prepare Korean meals for the travelers, meals that Alice found delectable.

The train was approaching Taiku, where the party was to spend the night in a Presbyterian mission. Possibly suspecting that the missionaries would not provide a cocktail hour, one of the party had fixed himself a whiskey and soda. Suddenly the train braked, and the drink spilled . . . on Alice. There was nothing to do. The train stopped at Taiku and they were expected to get off. Alice gathered up her things and proceeded down the aisle and then the steps, reeking of alcohol, to be greeted by their Presbyterian hosts. Just then, her cigarette case slipped from her hands, fell to the ground, and opened as it did, spilling cigarettes freely. Years later, telling a friend about the incident, she said, "So I arrived in an atmosphere of alcohol and tobacco which was thought deplorable, considering who our hosts were to be. But I do not think our hosts minded in the least. They were exceptionally nice, interested in everything that was going on."[419]

The train eventually deposited them in Fusan on the Korean coast. From there they traveled on a Japanese steamer to Shimonseki, Japan, where they transferred to a Canadian Mail steamer that carried them through the Inland Sea to Yokohama. For this visit to Japan as ordinary citizens, the Griscoms had once again invited Alice to stay at the legation, and as she toured, Alice was hoping to recreate the feeling she'd had when reading Japanese fairytales "in small crinkly books that I had had as a child."[420]

This time there would be no waving of American flags, no cheers, and, assuredly, no *banzai*s.

10

Tsu Shima Strait: Battle's Ghosts

Now that he'd established contact with the Japanese officials who would make the decisions about the Manchurian railway, Harriman wanted to see this railroad that the Russians had built. Before he made any final arrangements for the line's future operations, he needed to have a look at its tracks and rolling stock. E. H. Harriman and his family, friends, and retainers were on their way to Port Arthur at Manchuria's southern tip.

Leaving behind their social responsibilities with new Japanese friends, the Harriman entourage could look forward to a few days of being at least somewhat carefree. Their voyage through the Inland Sea, Tsu Shima Strait, and the Yellow Sea would require only the capacity to enjoy.

When they arrived in Kobe, they learned that, while they'd been in the midst of riots in Tokyo, there'd been rioting in Kobe as well. Protesters had attached a rope to a statue of Hirobumi Ito, pulled it down, and dragged it through the streets.[421] But now all seemed serene. At the docks in Kobe, their chartered steamer waited. To Cal McKnight, *Ohio III* appeared no larger than a fair-sized yacht. (By an interesting coincidence, it bore the same name as *Ohio II*, the U. S. warship that had transported Alice Roosevelt and her friends from China to Korea.) The travelers and their luggage went aboard, the crew cast off the lines, and the smokestacks and cranes of the industrial port soon fell behind them.[422]

They would be transiting Japan's Inland Sea, sheltered from the Pacific by the islands of Honshu and Shikoku. From the ship's decks, the travelers could see the islands' hills and mountains, rising in endless procession ahead of them, one behind the other, in soft, diminishing shades of blue-gray. To McKnight, the hundreds of islands and islets seemed to him like rugged versions of the Thousand Islands in the St. Lawrence River.

While much of Japan was laboring to catch up to the modern world, the islands of the Inland Sea were much as they had been for centuries past. Simple wooden houses with roofs of black or gray tile clustered to make up tiny villages. In many places, terraced fields climbed the hills behind them. Orchards contrasted with expanses of open pasture. Some islands were cloaked in pine woods while farm fields checkered other tiny islets. Here and there, the ragged remnants of old castles appeared, reminders of centuries of feudalism and conflicts among the warlords.

Each island had its own religious shrine, often requiring a climb of many steps for the faithful. Leading to the shrine from the water would be a huge gate, or "torii," painted a brilliant red, welcoming spirits of the departed as they came to the shrine across the Inland Sea.

Some fishing villages had miniature spirit houses set just above the level of the water, dedicated to whatever gods protected fishermen and brought them safely home. The travelers could see the fishermen themselves in their small boats, casting their nets for sea bream and prawns. Others set their pots for octopus.

There would be no time for stopping at any of these enchanted isles. Though there may have been some wistful glances toward the islands from its decks, *Ohio III* steamed past determinedly. Harriman was focused on his plan to investigate the condition of the South Manchurian Railway.

Harriman's inspection of the railway would be no casual visit. Those in charge could expect penetrating questions on subjects to which they may not have given much thought. On his first tour of the Union Pacific after gaining control, Harriman had left behind him scores of wrung-out railway officials, exhausted by his questions about tracks, cars, stations, switches, the route, the grades, curves, and geology.

He left the actual running of the trains to the men who did the work, but his eye for detail was legendary. During one of his early trips on the Union Pacific, he was puzzled by the long stop for the train to take on water. When he asked one of the crewmen what size pipe was used, he was told it was four to six inches. When Harriman asked why they used those particular sizes, the crewman replied that it was because that was the size they'd always used.

Harriman ordered that they change to twelve-inch pipe for taking on water throughout the system, and from then on Union Pacific trains saved significant amounts of time in their watering operations.[423] In Manchuria, Harriman would ask questions to help him to assess damage and estimate the cost to bring the line into operating condition.

When *Ohio III* reached the southernmost point of Honshu, the ship turned west and slipped through Kanmon Strait into the exposed waters of Tsu Shima Strait. Typhoon season was upon them, and they had several hundred miles of open water to cross. Should a storm overtake them, they would be decidedly uncomfortable in their small ship.

It was only four months earlier when, in these very waters, Japanese naval forces had discovered the ships of the Russian Second Pacific Squadron attempting to pass undetected through Tsu Shima Strait.

The Russians had lost fifty times as much shipping tonnage as the Japanese. Nearly five thousand Russian sailors had been lost and six thousand were taken prisoner. Some of these prisoners were the ones with whom Harriman had chatted when he visited the temples in Kyoto.

By contrast, the Japanese had lost 110 men.[424]

The Russians had made the mistake of thinking they were dealing with a small, unsophisticated island nation—for many years isolated from the rest of the world—and a nation whose ships would be no match for the mighty Russian navy. In any case, the battle of Tsu Shima Strait changed the way the rest of the world thought about Japan. No longer an insignificant minor power, Japan was now a major player on the Pacific scene.

As *Ohio III* and the Harriman crew plowed purposefully across Tsu Shima Strait, they passed through waters that only a few months before had been awash with the bodies of combatants; waters that flowed above the carcasses of once fearsome battleships.

Gentle winds and clear skies guided them, and the passengers could relax . . . all except Cal McKnight, who was suffering with a toothache. He'd have to possess his soul in patience until they reached their first port of call, Dalny, on the southernmost tip of Manchuria, still several days away. He could only hope there would be a dentist there.[425]

11

Port Arthur: War's Remains

Ohio III waited outside Port Arthur's harbor for its tug escort. Meanwhile, the Americans had just learned that, only a few days before, a Japanese transport had exploded when it hit a mine just outside the harbor, in waters they were about to pass through.[426] Would they hit a mine? And if they did, what then? In September 1905, navigating the harbor entrance at Port Arthur was a stomach-churning process.

Early in the war, just before they abandoned their naval base at Port Arthur, the Russians larded the harbor entrance with explosives.[427] Though the war was officially over, the devices had not been cleared. Now, *Ohio III* waited for a launch to guide the ship safely (the passengers sincerely hoped) through to the inner harbor.[428]

Before they left San Francisco, most of *Ohio III*'s passengers no more expected to disembark in Manchuria than they expected to drop by balloon into central Kyrgyzstan. Manchuria was not a tourist destination. Its ambiance lacked appeal: torrid summers followed by arctic winters; few cities; a sparse population; and a paucity of amusements. In the seventeenth century, even the native Manchus had eschewed its delights and relocated to China proper, where they eventually ruled the country.

Manchuria, however, was not without its charms for the industrially minded. It had coal and other minerals. It had railroads to transport the coal. It had arable land. It had Dalny, a warm-water commercial port.

And, though it was nominally governed by China, Chinese governance was distinguished mainly by its absence. The power vacuum in Manchuria, allowed by the Manchus' lack of oversight, had tempted the Russians to move aggressively to secure the leases that allowed them to build railroads and ports.[429]

Russia's incursions across Manchuria's long border with Korea had precipitated the war between the Japanese and the Russians. These Americans were about to see the place where the war's fiercest land battle had been fought.

Five days after leaving Kobe, *Ohio III* docked briefly in the port of Dalny, Manchuria, on the Liaodong peninsula, which thrusts itself into the northern extension of the Yellow Sea. Warehouses ringed the commercial port, which had been the supply hub for Japanese war operations.

Harriman and his friends were expected in Port Arthur the following day and planned to go there by train. When that wasn't possible, they re-boarded their little freighter and departed at six the next morning. Mercifully, during the brief stop, Cal McKnight had found a dentist to treat his aching tooth.

The trip to Port Arthur was short, but the wind kicked up a choppy sea, making the passengers uncomfortable. Outside the port, they had to wait for the harbor launch.

When the launch finally arrived, *Ohio III* followed cautiously and uneventfully in its wake to the inner harbor, where a scene of utter destruction opened up before them.

"Torpedo boats, steamships, tugs are strewn over the beaches, while masts and smokestacks jutting up through the water indicate where others are lying on the bottom," McKnight wrote to his wife. "In all, more than seventy-five vessels have been destroyed in the harbor and around the entrance. [The Japanese] are working on the best ones, raising and repairing them where possible. Yesterday they succeeded in raising the battleship Retvizan, which was the flagship of the Russian squadron."

The Harrimans and their party were the first foreigners to be allowed into the former Russian naval base since the end of the war, and *Ohio III* was flying the first U.S. flag seen there since the war's beginning. Japanese government officials were anxious to see that Harriman was treated well, and a delegation of army and navy officers greeted them. "You will be taken to see the battlefields," the officers explained. Horses were provided for those who wished to ride, and what McKnight described as "curious weather-beaten Russian carriages" awaited the others.

Their guide was a young Japanese army lieutenant who had taken part in the desperate fighting. The Japanese had been unable to take the Russian fortification at Dragon Hill by means of a frontal assault, and instead dug a tunnel in which they were able to detonate explosives. The lieutenant had been the second man to get inside the Russian position.[430]

At 203-Meter Hill, a key Russian defense position, they viewed the last point captured before the Russian surrender and the site of the fiercest fighting of the war. For the Japanese, the price of victory was incredibly steep: at least twenty thousand killed and thirty thousand wounded. They threw twenty-two thousand tons of projectiles at the fort before it was captured, the guide told them.

Their guide explained that, during the battle, the Japanese and Russian trenches were so close that when the Russians threw hand grenades down on the Japanese, the Japanese would catch them and hurl them back at the Russians before the lighted fuse could burn down. Thousands of combatants died on the side of the hill and were buried in shallow trenches where they fell.[431]

The tour of the battlefield was sobering, particularly for Harriman's thirteen-year-old son, Roland. In his memoirs seventy years later, he recalled that as they wandered around the battlefield, they could see many bodies not completely buried, "with arms and legs sticking above the ground."[432]

Following the tour, Harriman entertained the Japanese officers for lunch aboard *Ohio III*. In return, he and the other gentlemen in the party were invited by General Idichi, Port Arthur's commander-in-chief, for dinner at the Port Arthur Club, previously dedicated for use by Russian officers. Portraits of the tsar and Russian generals, flanked by Russian flags, gazed somberly down upon the guests. Russian silverware graced the table, and Russian coats-of-arms adorned the diners' plates.

"In fact, everything we used during our stay was Russian. The horses we rode, the carriages, the launches . . . the whole outfit," McKnight noted in a letter.[433]

Back in Tokyo, Griscom was working with Japanese officials to work out an arrangement whereby Harriman would supply the funds to put the Manchurian railroad back into operating condition. Harriman's financial group and the Japanese government would share control.[434] Now that Harriman had the bones of a workable plan between his teeth, his nature was to persevere for as long as it took to see it properly executed. He couldn't know that conditions beyond his control were about to make it hard to hang on to his plan.

12
Peking: Brief Interlude

Even as he walked into Taku's Ton Gau Railway Station in an unfamiliar country whose language he didn't speak, McKnight could sense that something was up—railroad personnel were edgy and excitement buzzed. An imperial special train would be arriving shortly from Peking. Someone who spoke English explained that the empress had appointed a group of special commissioners to go abroad to study successful programs and reforms in other countries that might be applied to situations in China. The train was to bring the commissioners from Peking to the port of Taku, where they would board the ship for the start of their mission. When the train failed to arrive at the scheduled time, railway officials expressed dismay. What was wrong? Why hadn't the train arrived as expected?

The Harriman group thought no more of the incident until, at the end of their 150-mile journey, they alighted from their train in Peking. Without a word of Chinese, they could still recognize distress when they heard it. Something bad had happened. The imperial special had not arrived in Ton Gau because an unknown person had hurled a bomb into a compartment of the special train just as it was about to depart from the station in Peking.

McKnight found someone who spoke English and was told that the bomb had killed four and wounded five of the commissioner's party.

The theory was that the culprit was a Chinese xenophobe or someone opposed to reform.

As McKnight described it when he wrote to May, there was "a belief that the affair was part of a well-organized plot in the higher official circles to prevent further injection of foreign ways and methods in China. We began to wonder if we were again to be in a storm center as at Tokyo."[435]

In Peking, there was no official welcome, there were no planned dinners or entertainments, and there were no translators to explain the surrounding scenes. Transportation on the unpaved streets varied from two-wheeled carts to camel trains. McKnight hired a cart for a drive around the city and saw men in long straight robes or trousers topped with simple tunics. He found Peking quaint and interesting but no match for Tokyo in the matter of cleanliness. With no plans, he ended up back in the hotel lobby, chatting with two American reporters to pass the time.[436]

While the Harriman family was in Peking, young Roland decided to slip out of their hotel to see a bit of the city on his own. What he described later were "dusty streets, with beggars all over the place." He bought some dates from a street-side seller and ate them on the spot. As an adult, years later, he still wondered why he had not come down with some dreadful affliction.[437]

Harriman wanted his family to see Peking's Sacred City. Alice Roosevelt and her friends had been the first foreigners to be granted permission. Now, E. H. Harriman was asking to be granted the same privilege.

Minister Rockhill had gracefully facilitated the arrangements for the visit of the president's daughter but did not offer much hope that Harriman's proposal would receive official approval. Harriman was not accustomed to being frustrated. When Rockhill proved correct and permission was denied, Harriman believed Rockhill had not persevered as he should have (or as Harriman would have) and threatened to take up the matter with the State Department. He never did.[438]

PART VII

WINDING DOWN

October 1905

1

Seoul: Unexpected Attraction

Three days in Peking had proved sufficient for the Harriman entourage. They boarded *Ohio III* once more to cross the Yellow Sea to Chemulpo, where a special train—the Japanese had been running Korea's railroads—carried them to Seoul. Edward Morgan, the American minister to Korea, welcomed the Harriman family as his guests at the legation, while a hotel and boarding house sheltered the others in the party.[439]

The visitors were hard on the heels of Alice Roosevelt and her friends, and Willard Straight was about to reprise his role as social director. A part of the entertainment that required no effort on his part was the legation's next-door neighbor, who turned out to be Korea's emperor himself. The visitors could look out from the legation at the lilting double roof line of the emperor's palace silhouetted against mountains north of the city. The emperor, however, was living in another building in the part of his compound overlooked by the U.S. legation.

For reasons known only to the initiated, the Korean government conducted business throughout the night. Should any of the Americans have been looking toward the palace compound at two or three in the morning, they would have seen the comings and goings of peculiar-looking (to American eyes) visitors draped in filmy gauze gowns and wearing tall hats with straight brims.

During the day, from their chairs on the legation verandah, the Americans might catch a glimpse of the diminutive emperor himself, trying to see what his Japanese gardener was up to. One of the emperor's concubines, Lady Om, had produced a son, whom the legation staff had dubbed "the omelette," and once in a while, a eunuch would hold up the infant "omelette" so he, too, could see what he could see.[440]

They saw the emperor in a more formal setting when he invited the Harrimans to a luncheon at the palace. A garden party arranged by Japanese officials found them strolling among the bamboo, old trees, lush evergreens, and stone lanterns of a Korean garden artfully planned to appear totally natural.[441]

For Willard Straight, the arrival of the Harrimans would play a part in the unrolling of both his career and his personal life. Harriman and Straight spent some time getting to know one another. It was easy to be impressed with this capable young man who could speak Chinese and had connections in China, Japan, and Korea. Few Americans had Straight's qualifications, and Harriman sensed that Straight's talents could make him a useful cog in any Asian business operation.[442]

As he shepherded the Harriman family through the Seoul festivities, Straight became aware of young Mary Harriman, and she of him. Mary had been away from friends her own age for two months, and except for her siblings, had been surrounded by her seniors. Now here was someone close to her own age, but more importantly, someone very different from the idle young men back home who had failed to attract her. Besides his open, unstudied manner, Straight had purpose—he was working for his country, after all—he was a talented artist, and he was hoping to be part of some as-yet-unspecified American enterprise in Asia.[443]

Seoul, Korea was a most unlikely place for fate to thrust these two Americans together: the petite, attractive, socially aware brunette and the fair-haired, lanky, talented, ambitious diplomat. Straight and Mary were both trying to reach beyond the limits that society prescribed for them. Each experienced the inchoate feeling that they were meant to be actors in meaningful events. They spent only a brief time together, but in that exotic setting, it was not surprising that they reached out to one another, going to formal parties, horseback riding, and laughing together. The relationship sparked.

According to her younger brother, Mary Harriman loved company, loved to dance, and loved to have fun.[444] Mary's difficulty was that, like Alice Roosevelt, she was expected to choose a husband within certain parameters. Wealthy fathers tended to be suspicious of penniless suitors for their daughters' hands. Mary's father expected that the man she married would have substantial money, either inherited or earned. Willard Straight was not a fortune-hunter, but he had no objection to marrying a wealthy woman. He had become used to moving in the upper levels of society, and marrying money would assure that he could afford to continue.[445]

Mary could see that her father was impressed with Willard Straight, but would he accept Willard Straight as a suitor for her hand? Mary had a strong will, and when she didn't agree with her father, she said so. For his part, her father expected the truth from her. She wouldn't lie to him, but she wouldn't be completely open either. She decided not to tell her father about the budding relationship yet . . . a decision she might later come to regret.[446]

Because the Japanese would soon be taking over Korea's foreign policy, there would be no need for a separate U.S. ministry in Seoul; the legation was expected to close shortly and Willard would be returning stateside.[447] In the meantime, the two promised to write to each other. Mary could look forward to Willard's letters and to seeing him on his return.

When it was time for the Harrimans to leave, Straight accompanied Mary and the rest of the party aboard the special train for the trip to the southern coast.[448] He was there to wave goodbye when the rest of the party boarded a Japanese steamer for Nagasaki, Japan, headed east for the first time in two months.[449]

2

Tokyo: No Banzais Here

What a difference two months can make! When Alice arrived in Tokyo in early August, she'd been greeted with cheers and "Banzai!" at every turn. But now, although the riots had ceased, many in Japan continued to blame the U.S. and its president for what they perceived as unfair treatment under the Portsmouth treaty. They had expected the U.S. to be their ally in securing what they felt to be their just rewards for their wartime victories. When their expectations were not met, resentment of Americans festered.[450] If the subject of their nationality came up when they were out in public, Alice and her friends were advised to say, "We're English."[451]

Alice and her friends took the short train ride to the seaside town of Kamakura to see the huge bronze statue of the Buddha, nearly fifty feet tall, about which Kipling wrote: "And whoso will, from Pride and/Contemning neither creed nor priest,/May feel the Soul of all the East/About him at Kamakura."[452] In contrast to their earlier time in Tokyo, when their every moment had been taken up by official events, their time on this visit was their own, and they were able to take in the sights at their leisure. As regular tourists, they traveled to Nikko to see the temples and the tombs of the Shoguns.[453]

Books had played a substantial role in Alice's upbringing—her father believed in reading to his children—and she had been charmed by

Japanese fairy tales, popular with English-speaking readers in the years of her childhood.[452] One story she'd read, *The Forty-Seven Loyal Ronins*, was based on an actual event. "Ronin" was a term for a samurai or warrior without a leader. The forty-seven were a group of warriors who had seen their leader, Asano, forced by the actions of another samurai, Kira, to commit seppuku (ritual suicide). The *ronins* had been unable to avenge their leader because Kira was too well guarded. For more than a year, the *ronins* pretended to become beggars and drunks, foregoing the code of the samurai, lulling Kira into believing that they would not try to get revenge. Finally, thinking he was safe, Kira dropped his guard. On December 15, 1702, the *ronins* attacked, captured Kira, and offered to let him commit seppuku. He refused. One of their number decapitated Kira, and they placed Kira's head on Asano's grave. Then, all forty-seven *ronins* committed suicide. They are buried next to their leader at Senkaku-ji Temple, overlooking Tokyo Bay. The story has been the subject of countless productions in Japanese theater.[453]

The story of the *ronins* became a favorite with the Japanese people, and the site of the *ronins*' graves became a place of pilgrimage and a destination for sightseers. Alice added herself to their number and basked in the feeling she'd had as a child, reading the story of loyalty even unto death.

In early October, the Harrimans and their entourage arrived back in Tokyo from Korea. In Manchuria, Harriman had learned that rebuilding the Russian-built railroad would mean laying miles of new track. Accordingly, the party had stopped in Nagasaki to investigate the capabilities of the city's steel works before going on to Yokohama for a bit of rest and their eventual return to Tokyo.[454]

The Harrimans' arrival meant the reunion of Mary Harriman and Alice Roosevelt. The Harriman and Roosevelt families had at one time lived only a few doors from one another on Manhattan's East 55th Street. Even though Mary Harriman was three years older than she was, Alice noted that Mary was her particular friend.[455] The two had arranged that Alice and her friends would join Mary and her family for the voyage back to San Francisco and then go on with them by train to New York. (Because Theodore Roosevelt was coming to regard E. H. Harriman as a corporate villain, it is possible that Alice had not consulted her father about these arrangements.)

While Alice had returned to play, Mary Harriman's father had come back to work. When he departed for Manchuria, Harriman had left Lloyd Griscom with the task of negotiating an agreement between Japanese officials and Harriman for their joint operation of the South Manchurian Railway, which the Japanese had acquired under the Portsmouth peace treaty. Time was growing short. Harriman was anxious to push ahead.

He wanted to have an agreement in hand. He wanted it immediately, before he sailed for the States. Japanese officials were astonished. Such haste was not a part of Japanese culture. The process went forward, nevertheless—a testimony to Harriman's persistence.[456]

To his surprise, Griscom found no serious opposition to the general idea of Harriman's proposal. The sooner the rebuilding was completed, the sooner part of the line's profits would accrue to the Japanese treasury, which had been seriously depleted by the costs of the war.

Count Katsura (the prime minister), admitted his favorable opinion of the plan to Griscom. So did Vice-Minister of Finance Saketani, and finally Count Inouye himself said, "We would be very foolish to let this chance slip."[457] The scale tipped when Harriman took part in the negotiations himself. He impressed his listeners with his confidence that he could make happen that which he was proposing. He said that he would make sure of it, and they believed him.

A memorandum of agreement was drawn, stating that a corporation would be organized under Japanese law. Though the corporation would purchase the track and equipment of the railway, ownership would be shared jointly with the Japanese. Similarly, the coal mines affiliated with the railway would also fall under shared ownership. The memorandum went on to say that Japan would initially control operations, but changes would be made from time to time so that the Japanese operators and the American financiers would be equally represented in management and would share control equally. Harriman believed that his U.S. associates would agree to the terms. J. Soyeda, president of the Japanese Industrial Bank, would be the communications link.[458]

For all the travelers, another onslaught of luncheons, dinners, and garden parties filled their final days in Tokyo. Although Americans were not popular with Japanese citizens, they were still at the top of the list with Japanese government and with the banking officials responsible for their country's financial well-being.

The president of the Bank of Japan hosted a luncheon in Harriman's honor at the Imperial Hotel.[459] They dined on lobster *Americaine*, *mousse de gibier* à *la financière*, filet mignon, and tendron of veal.[460] Matsuo, the host, proposed a toast to the health of Harriman and his party. In response, Harriman said, "I feel my incapacity to express to you our grateful recognition of your whole-souled welcome to and care of us during our visit, not only in your country but in the other countries which we have visited since we came to the Orient. We little expected to be taken up and carried along with so little friction and no trouble to ourselves." He went on to express his admiration for the capacity for organization and cooperation among the Japanese business community. He also praised the political and military leaders for their readiness to act and their willingness to concede, which had brought them to the attention of the entire world.

"It now devolves upon you to continue their methods by integrity of purpose and readiness to act by the same honest methods in dealing with other people, to show that you can and will meet the responsibilities which have devolved upon you by your acquisitions . . ."[461] Harriman, like the forceful parent that he was, apparently felt that the Japanese needed a bit of guidance as they took on the role of colonial power. Or perhaps, when he was in Korea, he had seen some of what Willard Straight was seeing: a view of the Japanese character not quite congruent with that of his gracious and thoughtful Tokyo hosts.

On another day, their host was Count Inouye, one of the Elder Statesmen, who entertained the group at a party set in his gardens at their October best—bright with scarlet maples and colorful blooming chrysanthemums. Prime Minister Katsura gave a luncheon for Harriman, at which Harriman expressed his appreciation for Lloyd Griscom, firstly for urging him to come to Japan and secondly for his "great tact and [the] many courtesies we have received at his hands."[462]

International finance, nostalgic touring, and garden parties were not the only occupations of the visitors. Foreshadowing the activities of later twentieth century Americans, these travelers of 1905 had been shopping. Cal McKnight was busy listing every package for stowage aboard *Siberia*.

The Harriman family luggage alone was staggering: steamer trunks; French trunks; hat trunks; clothes hampers; large trunks; small trunks; wicker baskets; hand bags. Add to that eighty-five boxes and packages containing everything from furs from Korea, boxes of silk, and a copper kettle, to a jade vase, bronze vases, ivory figurines, Japanese prints, a carving stand, and books. In addition, there were crates of wine, shells from the Port Arthur battlefield, furs from Peking, furs from China, a dragon (presumably not alive), and rugs, plus the boxes of unidentified contents from shops in Nikko and Kyoto.[463]

E.H. Harriman himself was taking back a unique gift from the Japanese officers at Port Arthur: a generous supply of old Napoleon brandy, captured from the Russians.[464]

Dr. Lyle had five boxes containing fencing suits, guns, fencing swords, and bows and arrows.

And in a startling turn, accompanying Cal McKnight back to the U.S. was Kimi, a young Japanese girl who was to be a nursemaid to

McKnight's three-year-old daughter Mary.[465]

Going back with Alice Roosevelt were the gifts from two empresses, the Sultan of Sulu, and others. Her Asian acquisitions were already creating a stir back in the States, with inquiries in the press about whether the gifts actually belonged to her or belonged to the U.S. government, since they were given to her as her country's representative.[466]

3
Tokyo: Gala Farewell

Looking around the crowded room, Lloyd Griscom could catch a glimpse of Hirobumi Ito chatting, E. H. Harriman conferring, and Prime Minister Katsura listening. The dinner was a farewell party: the traveling Americans would board *Siberia* tomorrow for the voyage back to the States. The ambiance was festive: silver glittered and crystal sparkled; the men were in evening black and white, their gleaming medals and colorful sashes contributing their own sparkle and luster; the women were in pale, artfully draped silks and satins that provided a softening, dramatic contrast. Because the Griscoms had learned early on to avoid white flowers unless the occasion were funereal, the flowers were determinedly colorful.[467]

Lloyd Griscom could be forgiven if he felt a bit of self-satisfaction mixed with a soupçon of relief. He'd been entertaining American visitors to Japan off and on for almost four months. And not just entertaining them—he thought back to the day he was to introduce the Taft group, individually, by name, to Japan's emperor. The trouble was that the group was made up of several dozen senators and congressmen he'd only met the day before. Only a certain amount of discreet whispering saw him through—not his smoothest performance.[468] During the riots, when protesters were wielding clubs and throwing rocks in the street, the responsibility for the safety of the Harriman party weighed heavily on him until they elected to leave town. Then there were the negotiations, always tedious, concerning the Manchurian Railways.

Harriman had wanted to reach a firm understanding with the Japanese government concerning the railways, and now, on his last full day in Japan, he finally had a signed memorandum of agreement in his pocket, reward for Griscom's skills and his own persistence.[469]

As for Alice Roosevelt, she had started with no clear goals in coming to the Far East other than to enjoy the general excitement of the adventure. But Griscom knew she'd gloried in the *banzai* cheers and being treated like an American princess. Theodore Roosevelt had believed that sending his daughter as his personal representative to Japan, China, the Philippines, and Korea would show U.S. interest in and respect for each of those countries. Alice could leave the hemisphere with the sense that she had been a credit to her father. Once she set foot on Far Eastern soil, she had extended herself to present an agreeable face to the public, forgoing the "conspicuous" activities that so perturbed her parents. She had been as charming as she knew how to be, and if she'd fulfilled her father's mission, that would be a step forward in their relationship. Because Alice was always open to the new and the different, another part of her reward had been the sheer joy of drinking in unaccustomed experiences in exotic locales. She would say, in later years, after many trips abroad, "The trip to the Far East was by far the most exciting one I ever made."[470]

Cal McKnight's future was still uncertain, but on September 3 he had written to his wife, "I don't know . . . what will be the result of this trip as far as the future relationship of Mr. H. and myself are concerned. I am sure he is satisfied with me, but I don't know that I am satisfied altogether with him."[471]

Lloyd Griscom knew he himself would not be in Japan much longer. He and Elsa were due for leave and the president had already announced his intention of appointing him to a new post. Before the status of "ambassador" had been created just a few years earlier, "minister" had been the top diplomatic category. The hope now was that an ambassadorship was in Griscom's future. Whatever the appointment turned out to be, it was clear they'd not be returning to Japan.[472] Tonight's gala farewell party for the Harrimans could be the beginning of their own Japanese swan song.

In terms of dignitaries on hand, the affair was supremely successful: the prime minister was present, along with several cabinet ministers and two of the *genro,* Count Inoue and Marquis Hirobumi Ito. Their presence was a testament to the quality of Griscom's diplomatic efforts, to the weight of Harriman's financial resources, and to the amplified U.S. presence in the Far East.

The party was ending. Earlier, Elsa and Lloyd Griscom had bid farewell to Alice, Nick Longworth, Mabel Boardman, Amy McMillan, the Newlands, and the Parsons. Now they said "goodbye" to the Harrimans, the Goelets, Cal McKnight, Dr. Lyle, and the be-medaled Japanese officials. It was a grand finale.

The Americans were officially leaving Japan.

4

Yokohama to New York: Homeward Race

Break the speed record between Yokohama and San Francisco? *Yes,* Harriman thought to himself, *the* Siberia *can make it happen.* When he voiced this thought to Robert Goelet, his friend disagreed.[473] Goelet felt the ship struggle up to the top of one wave and then slide down its backside, only to repeat the process, over and over. The shores of Tokyo Bay had faded away behind them, and wind and waves tumbled the ship without mercy, much like the first day of their outbound voyage from San Francisco.[474]

Siberia had to slow its pace. Given the adverse conditions, Goelet thought breaking the speed record was highly unlikely and said so to Harriman. That was enough motivation for Harriman. He proposed a wager: two thousand dollars to Harriman if, in spite of the difficult start, *Siberia* broke the record; and two thousand dollars to Goelet if it did not. Whoever won would donate his winnings to a seamen's charity.[475]

Robert Goelet was a twig on an old New York family tree, descended from Peter Goelet, a well-to-do New York City merchant. Robert had inherited a vast fortune, much of it in Manhattan real estate. He sat on the boards of several major banks and at least one railroad, was a patron of the Metropolitan Opera, belonged to a dozen or more exclusive clubs, and lived in a four-and-a-half-story brownstone mansion on Fifth Avenue. Robert Goelet was a very wealthy man.

For all of that, Goelet did not much care for losing money. With seas running high, he thought his money was safe. But when the wind subsided and the seas smoothed out, *Siberia* showed what it could do. The wager was a great diversion for the passengers, but when Goelet became extremely anxious as they drew close to the California coast, Alice couldn't resist a jab: "Have you paid some crewman to jump overboard so the ship will have to slow down?" she teased.[476]

When the ship steamed through the Golden Gate, *Siberia* had beaten the previous record by twenty-seven minutes. Goelet paid up. Harriman donated his winnings: half to those who worked in the engine room and half to the officers and crew.[477]

With the Pacific record in hand, Harriman decided to try for the San Francisco-East Coast record by train. Why not? He did control the railroad, after all. Consequently, when *Siberia* arrived in San Francisco Bay, the tugboat *Arab* pulled up alongside, gathered up the Roosevelt-Harriman group, and ferried them to the Southern Pacific terminal in Oakland on the eastern shore of the bay, completely bypassing San Francisco and disappointing the city's celebrity-watchers yearning for a glimpse of Alice Roosevelt. As they prepared to board their special train—made up of Harriman's private car as well as several sleeping cars and a dining car—Harriman received a mysterious communication from the local Japanese consul and tucked it away to read later.[478]

As the train attempted to cross the country faster than any train ever had, it sped through spectacular scenery. At Colfax, the track was embedded in the side of a canyon overlooking the American River, rippling more than a thousand feet below. The view was so amazing that trains would usually stop to allow passengers to relish the view, but this train had a speed record to break.

As they raced through the tunnels and snowsheds of the Sierra Nevada on the uphill grade to Reno, Harriman had time to digest contents of the cryptic note he'd received from the Japanese consul in San Francisco before they left Oakland. The note transmitted a message from Count Katsura, the Japanese prime minister:

The Japanese Government have found it necessary to institute a more thorough investigation and examination of the questions which are the subject of memorandum of October 12, 1905, and they consequently request you to regard the memorandum as in abeyance until they are able to communicate with you more fully regarding this matter.[479]

Only when Harriman arrived in New York would he discover the full implications of Count Katsura's brief communiqué.[480]

Meanwhile, on the train, the personages aboard had an opportunity to reflect on their own importance in the grand scheme of things as they passed expanses of mountain slopes girded with deep, green gorges that cradled rushing rivers, and the occasional lake that mirrored the firmament above. For three hundred miles, the train sped along the Humboldt River and then hurried through bleak Nevada mining towns, stopping only for fuel and water. The railroads had contracts to carry the U.S. mail, but in its rush across the country, Harriman's special train skipped the pick-ups.[481] Their non-stop mode also meant that Alice was spared the duty of standing on the train's rear platform and waving to the crowds waiting for a glimpse of the "American princess."

The train sped on into Utah and the Great Salt Lake, where the passengers could marvel as they rode the twelve-mile Lucan trestle that spanned the lake, dividing it in half. Only two years old, the wooden trestle was one of Harriman's upgrades, built to eliminate the extra mileage around the northern end of the lake and to reduce curvature in the track.[482] Less curvature meant that the trains could roll at higher speeds, a boon for a train in a rush to beat a speed record.

The Harriman train rocketed across Utah and into Wyoming, where it passed through Sherman, the highest point on their route at 8,013 feet above sea level. Newspaper headlines screamed: "Train Carrying Alice Roosevelt and E. H. Harriman Going Ninety Miles an Hour on a Downhill Grade to Omaha." (A railroad official noted that they were attempting to average speeds of forty to forty-five miles per hour. Harriman was hoping for fifty.)[483]

Theodore Roosevelt could read the headlines as well as anyone else, and once again, he didn't like what he saw. Although a railroad official denied it, legend has it that the president wired Harriman, ordering him to slow down. Harriman reportedly fired back, "You look after the country. I'll look after the railroad."

When they entered Nebraska, the Rockies fell behind them and the train shot across the plains that unrolled beneath the tracks. The Platte River meandered nearby, through territory laboriously crossed by wagon trains before the tracks were laid. Then it was on into Iowa, where the towns began to pass by more quickly, until finally the train crossed the mighty Mississippi River into Illinois.

Less than two hundred miles to go. Chicago would tell the tale—if they hadn't broken the record by then, it wasn't going to happen. The towns were coming thick and fast now, strung out along the route like beads on a necklace. Fulton . . . Union Grove . . . Morrison . . . Round Grove . . . Gate . . . Sterling . . . Nelson . . . Dixon . . . Nachusa . . . Ashton . . . Flagg. Chicago drew closer. Before long they were in the city's suburbs . . . West Chicago . . . Maywood . . . Oak Park . . . and finally Chicago!

Harriman's train had beaten the previous record by an amazing six hours, making the trip between Oakland and Chicago in fifty hours and forty-four minutes.[484] There was no time to explore Chicago's delights. Instead of stopping at the main terminal, the Harriman train was shunted off to the Lake Shore line and routed around the city. Because Nicholas Longworth was going to southern Ohio, his car was detached in Chicago, and he and Alice had to say farewell for the time being.[485]

The train averaged sixty miles an hour on the final leg between Chicago and New York. It finally pulled into Harriman, New York, (named after E. H.), forty-five miles north of Manhattan and the closest stop to Arden, the Harrimans' home. As the train came to a stop, the band cut loose with the "Star Spangled Banner," switching shortly to a rousing rendition of "Hail to the Chief." The park across from the station was lit with Japanese lanterns, and senior citizens and members of the athletic club and the jockey club had come out to say "welcome home" to the Harriman family.

Young Roland was first off the train, waving a banner given to him by his schoolmates before he left. His sisters and his parents remained on the train with Alice, Mabel Boardman, and Amy Macmillan until the train was ready to leave the station. When Alice finally appeared on the rear platform, she and her friends stood and waved handkerchiefs until the train pulled out of sight.[486]

The train continued on to Jersey City, across the Hudson River from Manhattan. Cal McKnight and Kimi alighted with all their luggage and headed for Bayside, Long Island, where McKnight's wife and daughter had been staying while he was away. Alice had arranged for a cab to meet her and her friends. She'd already sent a telegram addressed to "Mrs. Roosevelt, White House, Washington" that read: "Am on Harriman special. Impossible to make connections in Chicago. Will take eleven Friday train from Auntie Corrine's. Love, Alice."[487]

A police escort accompanied them as they took the ferry across the Hudson, where Alice would stay with her aunt in Manhattan. The next day, after an uneventful train trip from New York, Alice and her friends were back in Washington.[488]

Always good copy, Alice's name illuminated the headlines once more. On October 28, the day she arrived in Washington, a front-page headline announced, "Miss Alice Roosevelt Not About to Marry," with a subhead that added, "Denies She is Engaged to Anyone." (Alice wanted her parents to know before the headlines gave away the story.) The headline must have given pause to Secretary Taft, who had asked Alice while on the trip if she and Nick were engaged and was met with, "More or less, Mr. Secretary. More or less."

The speed record from Yokohama to New York belonged to the Harriman enterprises: the Pacific Mail Steamship company and the Southern Pacific and the Union Pacific railroad. And no other humans had ever made that journey faster than those in the Harriman-Roosevelt party.

The grand adventure was history.

EPILOGUE

Contrary to predictions, Japanese negotiator Baron Jutaro Komura was not assassinated on his return to Tokyo. A plot reportedly existed, but his friends, including Hirobumi Ito, spirited him from his ship to a safe place by an unpublicized route. When he learned of E. H. Harriman's plans for the Manchurian Railway in exchange for his financial backing, Komura lost his sorely tested patience. Enraged, he convinced officials that they should let only Japan profit from assets obtained through wartime sacrifice and painful negotiation. The Treaty of Portsmouth—the full text of which Komura had brought home with him—mentioned consulting with China on Manchurian matters. Given this rationale, the Japanese canceled the memorandum agreed to with Harriman.[489]

ꕥ

Hirobumi Ito went to Korea as the Japanese official in charge. In dealing with other Japanese officials, he urged that the Koreans be allowed to control their own destiny, but he was often overruled. In 1909, he was assassinated by a Korean man.[490]

ꕥ

Even though Count Sergei Witte had likely secured the most favorable terms for Russia, the Russian public gave him scant public recognition and dubbed him "Count Half-Sakhalin." Nevertheless, he was named head of the Council of Ministers (the equivalent of prime minister) and urged the tsar to allow democratic reforms.[491]

ꟼ

Willard Straight's life was directly affected by his contacts with Alice Roosevelt and the Harrimans. Soon after young Mary Harriman and her family returned from their Far Eastern trip, the Japanese completed their takeover of Korea. Willard Straight's job no longer existed—Korean diplomatic business was now conducted though the Japanese Foreign Ministry in Tokyo.[492] Straight returned to the States, where he and Mary found each other again. The romance flourished; they soon considered themselves engaged, but Mary kept the news from her father for more than a year. When he finally learned of it, Harriman was furious. He valued Straight as an adjunct to his business interests, but not, evidently, as a son-in-law. Since Straight had no record of business success, Harriman may have seen him as a fortune-hunter, but what bothered him most was that Mary had kept the engagement secret from him. Straight and young Mary ended their relationship.[493]

Following the Japanese takeover of Korea, Straight went to Cuba as Minister Morgan's secretary and deputy. In less than a year, the consular service transferred Straight from Cuba to Mukden, Manchuria as consul general. With his knowledge of the Chinese language, Straight was a natural for a Far Eastern post. He promoted U.S. interests in Manchuria until September 1908.[494]

Harriman kept in touch with Straight. He didn't want Straight for a son-in-law but valued him as a possible asset to his business. True to form, Harriman never abandoned his idea of a globe-girdling transportation network. In May 1909, Harriman joined a group of bankers who formed the American Group, a consortium attempting to obtain an interest in Chinese railroads. Straight immediately became the syndicate's agent in China, where he negotiated with government officials until the Chinese revolution intervened in 1912.[495]

ꕤ

The rift between Harriman and his once-good-friend Theodore Roosevelt continued to widen. The president had won favor with segments of the American public for his enforcement of the Sherman Anti-Trust Act. The act was intended to restrain cartels and monopolies from practices that resulted in restraint of trade, and to preserve a competitive marketplace for consumers. In 1904, Roosevelt's Justice Department had won a Supreme Court suit against Northern Securities under the Sherman Anti-Trust Act. E. H. Harriman was one of the founders of Northern Securities, and Roosevelt railed against Harriman and others he termed "malefactors of great wealth." His rhetoric reflected his conviction that Harriman was an arch-villain. Referring indirectly to John D. Rockefeller and Harriman, Roosevelt called them "the most dangerous members of the criminal class."[496]

He also struck the names of all the Harrimans from his Christmas card list.[497]

ꕤ

When Mabel Boardman returned to the States, she spearheaded fundraising for the endowment fund that put the American Red Cross on sound financial footing and enabled it to expand into local chapters around the country.[498]

In 1909, Mabel received a cable from Lloyd Griscom (then in Italy) asking for her help. The Sicilian city of Messina had been devastated by a massive earthquake followed by a tidal wave in Calabria. Thousands were homeless. Griscom organized relief efforts and delivered shiploads of supplies to the stricken city, but he needed more money and more supplies. Mabel and the American Red Cross took up the cause to raise funds for supplies.[499]

As longtime head of Red Cross volunteer services in the U.S., Mabel organized the training of nurses' aides and established the Red Cross home service, water safety program, Motor Corps, and Canteen Corps. She also established the Gray Ladies, volunteers who assisted hospital patients.[500]

☙

Elsie Clews Parsons had earned her PhD in sociology in 1899 and, in the year following the Far Eastern trip, published a textbook titled *The Family*, whose final chapter made headlines. Decades ahead of her time, Parsons suggested that early marriage should be discouraged. Instead, society should opt for trial marriage (without children). Trial marriage would allow postponement of monogamous marriage and allow individuals to be more mature when they became parents. The book was passionately condemned in pulpits and newspapers. After that, as long as her husband was in politics, Parsons used a pseudonym for her published material.

Parsons' interests widened, and from 1919 to 1941 she became, successively, president of the American Folklore Society, president of the American Ethnological Society, and the first woman president of the American Anthropological Association.[501]

☙

Lloyd Griscom continued in the diplomatic service. After he left Japan, he accepted an appointment as ambassador to Brazil. During a stopover in New York, he received a note from E. H. Harriman asking him to come to his office.

Harriman welcomed him warmly and told him he had just arranged Griscom's appointment as head of Harriman's New York office. Taken aback, Griscom stammered that he had just accepted the Brazilian ambassadorship and suggested that he would be of more value to Harriman as an ex-ambassador than as an ex-minister.

Harriman, genuinely puzzled that anyone would not immediately accept his offer, told Griscom, "The time to go into the business world is when somebody wants you."

Griscom turned down the job, and that was the end of that.[502]

Following his service in Brazil, Griscom was appointed ambassador to Italy, where he and Elsa enjoyed a princely lifestyle—provided, presumably, by money inherited from his family's shipping-line business. They spent time hobnobbing with King Victor Emanuel, his queen, and their family. While Griscom was ambassador to Italy, the Wright brothers arrived in Rome to demonstrate their new flying machine there. Griscom was awed. He gave the brothers no peace until they agreed to take him up. Wilbur flew the plane, which was made of slats, had no floor, and bore supports repaired with household twine and wire. The ten-minute flight, including a close encounter with a line of telegraph wires, seemed hours-long to Griscom. They flew at the amazing height of two hundred feet.

Shortly after the U.S. entered World War I in 1917, Griscom, by then an army major, found himself in France on the staff of John Pershing (who had been his military attaché in Tokyo). Now a major-general, Pershing commanded American forces in Europe. He shaped inexperienced troops into an army that could support French and British fighting units that were weary and depleted after three years of combat against a relentless German military force. Pershing sent in crucial reinforcements that helped turn the tide in favor of the allies. Until the end of his days, Pershing was regarded as a hero, both in the U.S. and Europe.[503]

ഗ

Four years after the Far Eastern trip, E. H. Harriman's health began to fail. He sought relief at an Austrian spa and was returning by way of Paris when Lloyd Griscom paid him a call. Griscom told him he was leaving the diplomatic service.

Harriman asked him what he wanted to do next.

"Direct a New York City newspaper," was Griscom's offhand reply.

"Which newspaper?" Harriman asked.

When Griscom said he'd have to look into the subject, Harriman told him to look into it and get back to him.

"I don't see why I shouldn't buy you a paper," Harriman added.

After they'd both returned to the U.S., Harriman asked Griscom to join him at Arden to discuss buying the paper, but the discussion never took place. Harriman's death on September 9, 1909, intervened.[504]

☙

Harriman left his fortune to his wife Mary, who managed it efficiently, devoting a portion of it to philanthropic causes. Among her altruistic endeavors, the senior Mary Harriman added thousands of acres to Bear Mountain and Harriman state parks on the west side of the Hudson River. She also continued to support the New York City Boys' Clubs, founded by her husband.[505]

☙

Averell, the Harrimans' older son, became a prominent figure on Wall Street. Early in World War II, he accompanied President Franklin Roosevelt when Roosevelt and Winston Churchill signed the Atlantic Charter, and during the war, Averell served as ambassador to the Soviet Union and to Great Britain. In 1954, he was elected governor of New York on the Democratic ticket and served one term. In the fifties, he was twice a candidate for the Democratic nomination for U.S. president.[506]

☙

Roland Harriman joined his older brother on Wall Street and became a successful stockbroker. A steadfast Republican, he carried on the family tradition of philanthropy. Shortly after World War II, President Truman appointed him president of the American Red Cross, where he served for twenty-three years.[507] Under his leadership, the American Red Cross developed the world's largest blood bank system.[508]

ᔓ

Young Mary Harriman married another artist, Charles Ramsey, but only after her father's death. She became a Democrat, and President Franklin D. Roosevelt appointed her chair of the consumer advisory board in the National Recovery Administration. She worked with farmers' cooperatives and encouraged the formation of consumers' rights groups.[509] She was killed in her thirties in a horseback-riding accident.[510]

ᔓ

Cal McKnight did not continue to work for E.H. Harriman when the trip was over. True to his reputation for discretion, he left no record of the reason for the parting. Instead, he joined his brothers' firm and became a developer of Long Island real estate.[511]

ᔓ

Kimi Ono, the young Japanese girl who accompanied Cal McKnight back to the U.S., became nursemaid to three-year-old Mary McKnight. When Mary outgrew the need for a nursemaid, Kimi went on to become companion to an elderly woman, traveling with her to such places as White Sulphur Springs. Kimi eventually returned to Japan, and Cal's wife, May, continued to correspond with her until the U.S. went to war with Japan in 1941. Then, they lost touch

ᔓ

Theodore Roosevelt won the prestigious Nobel Peace Prize for his success in bringing the warring Japanese and Russians face to face, and for his success in promoting the compromise that finally produced the Treaty of Portsmouth.

❧

William Howard Taft favored a congressional bill to lower the tariff on Philippine sugar, but congress did not reduce the tariff until 1909, while he was president, when it passed a bill that allowed the importation of up to three hundred thousand tons of Philippine sugar into the U.S. tariff-free.[512] By 1913, the Philippines was included in the U.S. customs zone and sugar became tariff-free.

The Philippines did not gain their independence until July 4, 1946.

❧

The Japanese continued their domination of Korea until the end of World War II. The country finally became independent of Japanese control on August 15, 1945, forty years after Taft's fateful conversation with Prime Minister Taro Katsura.

❧

In 1908, William Howard Taft was elected president of the U.S. In 1912, he and his once-good friend, Theodore Roosevelt, became estranged when they opposed each other for the Republican nomination. Taft secured the most votes in the convention and became the Republican candidate, but Roosevelt ran as the candidate of the Bull Moose Party. The Republican vote was divided, and Democrat Woodrow Wilson won in the general election. In 1920, Taft achieved his dream: he was appointed chief justice of the U.S. Supreme Court. He is the only person ever to have served as both president and chief justice of the United States.[513]

❧

Alice Roosevelt and Nicholas Longworth did indeed become engaged immediately after their return from the Far East. Four months later, on February 17, 1906, they were married in a grand White House wedding and decided to honeymoon in Cuba.[514] Meanwhile, Edwin Morgan had been appointed U.S. minister to Cuba and Willard Straight would again be his secretary and deputy. Straight went to Havana, acquired a legation building, furnished it, and staffed it before the others arrived. Straight, Morgan, Nick, and Alice moved in at the same time. Straight accompanied Nick and Alice on a triumphal tour of the island, whose inhabitants had warm feelings for Alice's father and his "Rough Riders" because they had helped liberate the island from Spanish rule.[515]

Secretary Taft proved right about the couple's prospects for happiness together when Nick's drinking and womanizing became issues. Although they remained married until Nick's death in 1931, each found solace in others: Nick with a string of mistresses; and Alice—when she was approaching forty—with Bill Borah, U.S. senator from Idaho.[516]

A hue and cry were raised throughout the U.S. over the gifts Alice received from the empresses and others, some claiming that they were really gifts to the American people. Alice retained possession but had to pay customs duty on them. Manchu, the Pekinese given her by Empress Cixi, remained with her for years.[517]

Alice and her father grew closer, and she became his ardent political supporter. She herself was never a public speaker, but the president knew she had her finger in the political wind, and he trusted her to critique his speeches before he delivered them.[518] Nick Longworth continued to serve his Ohio district in congress, and eventually became a popular speaker of the House of Representatives. Alice went regularly to the Capitol when the House was in session and followed all the legislation and political maneuvering. She blossomed into a political hostess—she seemed to know everybody. Unlike the haughty expression she wore in the formal portraits of her youth, broad smiles flashed when photographers approached for photos in her later years.

Alice Roosevelt Longworth died in 1980 but not before she'd become known as "the other Washington monument."[519]

ᔕ

Wedding bells rang for two other couples as a result of the trip. Bourke Cockran did not forget the lovely Ann Ide. On July 14, 1906, a Manila newspaper announced the engagement of Congressman Bourke Cockran to Annie Ide, daughter of now-Philippine Governor-General Ide. They were married the following November. At fifty-one, Cockran was twenty years Annie's senior.[520]

Mignon Critten, Alice's New York friend, had kept a low profile during their travels—perhaps because she had met someone who monopolized her time: Rep. J. Swaggart Sherley from Kentucky, a member of Taft's congressional delegation. The two were married April 21, 1906 at her family estate, Grymes Hill, on Staten Island.[521]

All told, three members of the U.S. House of Representatives indulged in matrimony after the journey ended. Some were calling Secretary Taft "Cupid."[522]

ᔕ

Most of the travelers never returned to the Far East. How the trip influenced their thinking is impossible to know. In the years that followed, a number of them were prominent in public life (see above), and it's safe to say that they brought to their tasks a perspective that few other Americans of the time could.

Venturesome souls, all.

PEOPLE OF REFERENECE

Lloyd Griscom – U.S. Minister to Japan

Elsa Griscom – wife of Lloyd Griscom

Alice Roosevelt – daughter of President Theodore Roosevelt

Edward Henry "E.H." Harriman – Wall Street financier, head of Union Pacific Railroad, Southern Pacific Railroad, and Pacific Mail Steamship Line

Willard Straight – secretary to the head of the Chinese Customs Service

Hirobumi Ito – one of the Japanese elder statesmen (*genro*), neighbor of Lloyd Griscom

Jutaro Komura – Japanese foreign minister, head of Japanese delegation to Portsmouth peace conference

Jack London – writer, journalist

Richard Harding Davis – writer, journalist

Theodore Roosevelt – 26th U.S. president

William Howard Taft – U.S. secretary of war (went on to become the 27th president of the U.S.)

George von Lengerke Meyer – U.S. ambassador to Russia

J. Calvin McKnight – confidential secretary to E. H. Harriman

Mary Averell Harriman – wife of E. H. Harriman

Mary Harriman – daughter of E. H. Harriman and Mary Averell

Averell and Roland Harriman – sons of E. H. Harriman and Mary Averell

Count Sergei Witte – head of Russian delegation to Portsmouth peace conference

Mabel Boardman – board member of the American Red Cross, friend of Alice Roosevelt

Lafayette Young – editor of *Des Moines Capital* newspaper

Nicholas Longworth – U.S. congressman from Ohio

Herbert Parsons – U.S. Congressman from New York

Elsie Clews Parsons – lecturer on sociology at Barnard College, wife of New York congressman Herbert Parsons

Robert Goelet – wealthy New York businessman, friend of E. H. Harriman

Bourke Cockran – U.S. congressman from New York, renowned orator

SOURCES

Note: In the endnotes, frequently used citations are identified by the initials indicated on this page. While the endnotes are in order of appearance in the book, these sources are in alphabetical order for easy reference.

MB1 Mabel T. Boardman, "A Woman's Impression of the Philippines," *Outlook Magazine*, vol. 82, Feb. 24, 1906.

MB2 _______________, "An Audience with the Dowager Empress of China," *Outlook Magazine*, vol. 90, Dec. 12, 1908.

JB James Bradley, *Imperial Cruise: A Secret History of Empire and War* (New York: Little, Brown and Company, 2009).

DB David Burton, *William Howard Taft, Confident Peacemaker* (Philadelphia: St. Joseph's University Press, 2004).

JC Jung Chang, *Empress Dowager Cixi: The Concubine Who Launched Modern China* (New York: Anchor Books, 2013).

Ken Chowder, *North to Alaska* (Smithsonian Magazine, June 2003).

SAC Stacy A. Cordery, *Alice: Alice Roosevelt Longworth, from White House Princess to Washington Power Broker* (New York: Penguin Group, 2007).

HC Herbert Croly, *Willard Straight* (New York: The Macmillan Company, 1924).

Baronne Eleanora Mary D'Anthethan, *Fourteen Years of Diplomatic Life in Japan* (London: Stanley Paul & Co., 1912).

RAE Raymond A. Esthus, *Double Eagle and Rising Sun: The Russians and Japanese at Portsmouth in 1905* (Durham: Duke University Press, 1988).

CF Carol Felsenthal, *Princess Alice* (New York: St. Martin's Press, 1988).

LG Lloyd Griscom, *Diplomatically Speaking* (New York: The Literary Guild, 1940).

RH Roland Harriman, *I Reminisce* (Garden City, New York: Doubleday & Company, 1975).

James Huffman, "The Meiji Restoration Era, 1868-1889," Japan Society, accessed Jan. 21, 2021, https://aboutjapan.japansociety.org/content.cfm/the_meiji_restoration_era_1868-1889.

GJ Geoffrey Jukes, *Russo-Japanese War (*Oxford: Osprey Publishing, 2002).

GK1 George Kennan, *E. H. Harriman: A Biography* (Boston: The Riverside Press, 1922).

GK2 George Kennan, *E. H. Harriman's Far Eastern Plans*, Reprint from the collection of the University of Michigan Library. Original document: 1917.

MK Maury Klein, *Life & Legend of E. H. Harriman* (Chapel Hill: University of North Carolina Press, 2001).

Lilla Licht and William Moore, *McKnight Genealogy* (New York: Lilla G. McKnight, Publisher, 1981).

SB Jack London, Edited by Stephen Brennan, *Autobiography of Jack London*, (Delaware: Skyhorse Publishing, 2013).

ARL Alice Roosevelt Longworth, *Crowded Hours* (New York: Charles Scribner's Sons, 1933).

AL Arthur Lubow, *The Reporter Who Would Be King: A Biography of*

Richard Harding Davis (New York: Charles Scribner's Sons, 1992).

Alison McKay, *Images of Bayside*, Bayside Historical Society (Charleston, S.C.: Arcadia Publishing, 2008).

JCMcK1 John Calvin McKnight, *Brief Record of a Trip to the Orient by Mr. E.H. Harriman and Party*, Papers of Averell Harriman, Library of Congress, 1905.

JCMcK2 ____________________, His journal, 1905, in author's possession.

JCMcK3 ____________________, Letters to May McKnight, 1905, in author's possession.

JCMcK4 ____________________, Miscellaneous papers, in author's possession.

Patrick McSherry, "The Army Transport Service," The Spanish-American War Centennial Website, accessed January 22, 2021, https://spanamwar.com/transports.htm.

EM Edmund Morris, *Theodore Rex* (New York: The Modern Library, 2001).

Rod Paschall, "Folly in the Philippines,"_HISTORYNET, accessed Jan. 21, 2021, https://www.historynet.com/arthur-macarthur.

JP John Pershing, *My Life before the World War, 1860-1917: A Memoir* (Lexington: University of Kentucky, 2013).

CP Constantine Pleshakov, *Last Armada* (New York: Basic Books, 2008).

David R. Rapkin, "The Emergence of U.S.-Japan Rivalry in the Early 20th Century," *Evolution of Great Power Rivalries* (University of South Carolina Press, 1999).

MT Michael Teague, *Mrs. L: Conversations with Alice Roosevelt Longworth* (Garden City, N.Y.: Doubleday & Company, 1981).

Howard Teichmann, *Life and Times of Alice Roosevelt Longworth* (New Jersey: Prentice-Hall, 1979).

EPT Eugene P. Trani, *Treaty of Portsmouth: Adventure in American Diplomacy* (Lexington: University of Kentucky Press, 1969).

AW Arthur Walworth, *Black Ships off Japan: Story of Commodore Perry's Expedition* (New York: Alfred A. Knopf, 1946).

LY Young, Lafayette, "Taft Hears All About Coolie Labor in Hawaii," *Des Moines Capital*, Aug. 25, 1905.

_______________, "Reception of Taft Party at Tokyo," Des Moines *Capital,* Aug. 30, 1905

_______________, "Stormy Days in the City of Manila," Des Moines *Capital*, Des Moines *Capital*, Oct. 26, 1905.

_______________, "Return of Taft Party to Manila," Des Moines *Capital*, Oct. 28, 1905.

_______________, "Farming in the Philippine Isles," Des Moines *Capital*, Oct. 30, 1905.

_______________, "Snobs of the Consular Service," Des Moines *Capital*, Nov. 4, 1905.

_______________, "Mr. Young Tells of His Conclusions," Des Moines *Capital*, Nov. 9, 1805.

_______________, "Snobs of the Consular Service," Des Moines *Capital*, Nov. 4, 1905.

RLZ Rosemary Levy Zumwalt, *Wealth and Rebellion* (Urbana and Chicago: University of Illinois, 1992).

ENDNOTES

Part I: Lifetime of Memories

Part II: Starting Something

1. Boston: Unwelcome Letter

1 In a fury, Alice . . . ARL, 61.
2 On a delightful summer . . . SAC, 65.
3 Because Alice was . . . ARL, 60.
4 It reminded her . . . ARL, 60.
5 In a group picture . . . MT, 52.
6 Alice smoked cigarettes . . . SAC, 77.
7 And it was generally . . . SAC, 65.
8 When she slit open . . . ARL, 61.
9 Her father enumerated . . . ARL, 61.
10 The latter was what stung . . . MT, 72.
11 She could recall . . . SAC, 70.
12 The very same girl . . . SAC, 70-71.
13 By this time . . . SAC, 71.

2. New York: Invitation Extended

14 Edward Henry Harriman was . . . GK, 1-2.
15 Elsa Griscom knew . . . LG, 223.
16 Conversation flowed . . . LG, 223.
17 The Griscoms certainly . . . MK, 285.
18 The son of an Episcopal minister . . . MK, 31.
19 He'd tangled with . . . MK, 65.
20 . . . he'd taken over . . . MK, 118.
21 . . . he'd acquired control . . . MK, 284.
22 The Far East looked . . . GK, 3-4.
23 As the highest-ranking . . . LG, 220.
24 The evening went well . . . LG, 223.
25 Harriman was to railroads . . . MK, xiii.
26 At only five feet . . . MK, 44.
27 Roosevelt, Griscom thought . . . LG, 223.

28 As Alice Roosevelt put it . . ." Brainy Quotes, accessed January 13, 2021, https://www.brainyquote.com/quotes/alice_roosevelt_longworth_115487#.
29 Harriman, on the other . . . LG, 223.
30 But Griscom realized that . . . LG, 223.
31 As the dinner party ended… LG 223.

3. Tokyo: War's Onset
32 Lloyd Griscom needed to…LG 229.
33 Japanese diplomats tended…LG 229.
34 When they'd arrived . . . LG, 225.
35 Next door to the U.S. . . . LG, 227.
36 Once, early on in . . . LG, 235
37 Their guests appeared . . . LG, 235.
38 Years later, in his memoirs . . . LG, 235.
39 Hirobumi Ito, Griscom's neighbor . . . GJ, 12.
40 On February 6, 1904 . . . LG, 240-241.
41 On February 9, 1904 . . . GJ, 24-26.
42 And because the Japanese . . . LG, 240, 238.

4. Tokyo: Painful Parting
43 "For the Rosens . . ." LG, 242.
44 Seeing Baron and Baroness Rosen . . . LG, 242.

5. Peking: Career Change
45 Swinging incense burners . . . HC, 105-110.
46 Straight was taken aback . . . HC, 108.
47 For a while . . . HC, 65.
48 His ingenious pranks . . . HC, 26.
49 Tokyo's sights impressed . . . HC, 27.
50 The Boxer Rebellion had . . . HC, 77.
51 He and the other . . . HC, 79-80.
52 Over this time . . . HC, 111.

6. Tokyo: Restive Reporter
53 When the flames of war . . . LG, 245.
54 Martin Egan, the personable . . . HC, 145.
55 They were men . . . LG, 245.
56 The many reporters . . . HC, 125-126.
57 One day, however . . . Dale L. Walker, "Jack London, War Correspondent, on the Russo-Japanese War" The Accidental Aanarchist, accessed February 5, 2021, https://theaccidentalanarchist.com/jack-london-war-correspondent-on-the-russo-japanese-war/.
58 He'd arrived aboard . . . Mancini, See note 56.
59 His good looks . . . AL, 4-5.
60 The product of a . . . SB, 9.
61 In Tokyo, he . . . Mancini, See note 56.

62 After London left . . . Mancini, See note 56.
63 Despite Griscom's pleas . . . LG, 246.
64 The story made the rounds . . . Mancini, See note 56.
65 Richard Harding Davis was . . . LG, 250.

7. Washington: Anxious Romance
66 "No young woman . . ." ARL, 46-47.
67 Nick was interesting . . . SAC, 104.
68 But experience had taught . . . SAC, 16-17.
69 Alice's unease about . . . SAC, 105-6.
70 "I was brought up . . ." MT, 70.
71 She didn't set out . . . MT, 70.
72 There were rumors . . . AC, 77.
73 And a photographer . . . MT, 81.
74 Alice and her father . . . MT, 77.
75 One of her friends . . . MT, 74.
76 Always careful to . . . MT, 75.
77 That February in . . . "New York City: Lowest Temperature for Each Year," Current Results, accessed January 13 2021, https://www.currentresults.com/Yearly-Weather/USA/NY/New-York-City/extreme-annual-new-york-city-low-temperature.php.
78 . . . but Alice effectively smashed . . . SAC, 56-57.
79 Now it was March 4 . . . ARL, 67-68.

8. Washington: Offer Accepted
80 The president's diplomatic . . . RAE, 26.
81 If Theodore Roosevelt had . . . RAE, 47.
82 Then again, his anxiety . . . RAE, 17.
83 Because Secretary of State . . . EM, 378.
84 Japanese foreign minister . . . EPT, 52.
85 . . . while Count Cassini . . . EM, 378.
86 Neither side would . . . EPT, 30-31.
87 The president decided . . . EM, 378.
88 The president was tired . . . EM, 379.
89 In April, the snows . . . EM, 381.
90 At night as he . . . EM, 383.
91 On April 26 . . . EM, 382.
92 Meanwhile, his absence . . . EM, 384-385.

9. Albany: Uncertain Future
93 "A good organizer . . ." *Mercantile and Financial Times*, Chicago, Mar. 25, 1905.
94 A Confidential secretary . . . Mary McKnight Malmar, Cal McKnight's daughter, in conversation with the author.
95 When Odell's term . . . *New York Evening Post,* Feb. 16, 1905.
96 A New York Paper . . . Newspaper clipping, unidentified.

97 When his family moved . . . *The Globe,* date unknown.
98 The oldest, Stewart . . . Lilla McKnight and William Moore, *McKnight Genealogy* (Lilla McKnight Publisher, 1981).
99 McKnight went to work . . . Alison McKay and Bayside Historical Society, *Bayside* (Arcadia Publishing, Charleston, S.C. 2008).
100 When Odell himself . . . "Dinner to Mr. Odell; He Advocates a Shipbuilding Plant, and Offers to Take Stock in It," *The New York Times,* Dec. 1, 1900, accessed January 14, 2021, https://www.nytimes.com/1900/12/01/archives/dinner-to-mr-odell-he-advocates-a-shipbuilding-plant-and-offers-to.html.
101 "I'll look out . . ." JCMcK3, date unknown.

10. Washington: Dilemmas Resolved
102 Congressmen from sugar . . . "The Philippine Sugar Tariff," *Aspen Daily Times,* Jan. 10, 1905.
103 The Filipinos, on . . . "Philippines Tariff Appeal," *The New York Times*, January 1, 1905, accessed January 14, 2021, https://www.nytimes.com/1905/01/01/archives/philippines-tariff-appeal-save-us-from-ruin-the-cry-by-lifting.html.
104 He also knew . . . DB, 30-31.
105 But Roosevelt believed . . . EM, 110.
106 A plan was already . . . DB, 46.
107 While publicly neutral . . . ET, 28.
108 If there were to be . . . ET, 85.
109 William Howard Taft . . . DB, 20.
110 Taft preferred the . . . DB, 23.
111 He had a reputation. . . DB, 13.
112 At one time . . . DB, 14.
113 Later, as a federal . . . DB, 20-23.
114 When President McKinley . . . DB, 23.
115 Taft did well in the . . . DB, 32.
116 But it was the measures . . . DB, 33-34.
117 And Alice . . . he would . . . ARL, 68-69.

Part III: Preliminaries, June 1905

1. Tokyo: Turning Point
118 Tsar Nicholas made . . . GJ, 71-73.
119 In Tokyo, the Griscoms . . . LG, 253-254.

2. St. Petersburg: Skillful Diplomat
120 The minister's diplomatic . . . EM, 389-390.
121 Finally, Meyer read . . . EM, 390.
122 Back in St. Petersburg . . . EM, 389-391.

3. New York: Decision Made
123 He had also . . . MK, 219, 284.
124 Thus, Harriman currently controlled . . . MK, 284-285.

125 Japan looked likely . . . RAE, 19.
126 Jacob Schiff, Harriman's . . . MK, 284.

4. New York: Travel Plans
127 Six years earlier . . . MK, 183-200.
128 By the time the ship . . . JCMcK1, 1.

5. New York: Shortage of Prospects
129 "Mary loved company . . ." RH, 6.
130 Few girls at the turn . . . MK, 299.
131 Mary was only nineteen . . . "Celebrating Mary Harriman and the NYJL," *Junior League Magazine*, accessed January 15, 2021, https://www.nyjl.org/celebrating-mary-harriman-and-the-nyjl/.
132 Bertie Goulet, the son of . . . MK, 302.

6. Seoul: Adventure's Promise
133 Being a war correspondent . . . HC, xii.
134 Even as his feet hit the dock . . . HC, 125.
135 Once, when his mother . . . HC, 26-27.
136 Now as an adult . . . HC, 142-146.
137 When officials finally . . . HC, 130.
138 With time to look . . . HC, 127.
139 A short time later . . . HC, 152.
140 Pershing, a West Point . . . JP, 151, 166.
141 In Manchuria, the ex-cavalryman . . . JP, 226.
142 The war stalled . . . JP, 229, 231.
143 Straight, meanwhile, had . . . HC, 150.
144 Making his way south . . . HC, 149.
145 While Straight was . . . HC, 135.
146 Soon after, Morgan . . . HC, 155.

7. Pine Knot: Rural Respite
147 She'd found a simple . . . EM, 392.
148 They had traveled . . . EM, 391.
149 "It is really . . ." "Virginia: Where Presidents Go to Get Away from It All," *Richmond Times Dispatch*, June 18, 2017.
150 President Theodore Roosevelt's ability . . . EM, 392.

8. Washington: Rising Excitement
151 He must have *some* . . . JC, 3.
152 She did so want . . . CF, 77.
153 But Alice knew that . . . CF, 85.
154 Longworth was experienced . . . SAC, 100-105.
155 Alice, however, was unsure . . . SAC, 128.
156 Warm weather had . . . SAC, 114.
157 She was pleased . . . MT, 41.

158 Thoughts about Nick . . . CF, 114.
159 Because "Uncle Will" Taft . . . CF, 114.
160 For formal occasions . . . ARL, 74.
161 Missing, however, was . . . MT, 118.
162 The carefully folded . . . ARL, 74.
163 "My darling girl . . ." SAC, 112.

Part IV: Underway, July 1905

1. San Francisco: Westward Ho!
164 Alice Roosevelt was . . . ARL, 72.
165 Several days earlier . . . ARL, 70.
166 Edith Newlands was . . . ARL, 73.
167 "I had a little atlas . . ." ARL, 70.
168 Schwerin graciously offered . . . ARL, 71.
169 Too, she was well acquainted . . . ARL, 69.
170 Alice claimed she was so excited . . . ARL, 70-71.
171 Newspapers reported that . . . ARL, 73.

2. Pacific: At Sea
172 "Our bustling and shapeless . . ." RLZ, 69.
173 In a letter to his wife . . . RLZ, 69.
174 In fact, thirty-one-year-old . . . RLZ, 7-9.
175 She was a stalwart supporter . . . RLZ, 7-9, 67.
176 Elsie's husband was. . . RLZ, 71.

3. Washington: Obstacles to Peace
177 Each side had listed . . . EPT, 62-67.
178 Because of the decisive . . . EPT, 91.
179 But Roosevelt had heard . . . RAE, 61.
180 Their concern was well-founded . . . RAE, 52.
181 The president continued . . . RAE, 52.
182 At the same time . . . RAE, 53.
183 In early July, Roosevelt . . . EM, 124, 125.

4. New York: Job Offer (While the book's setting of this section took place in Harriman's office, the specific location of the site was never recorded.)
184 Cal McKnight hoped . . . JCMcK3, 1905.
185 McKnight thought . . . JCMcK3, 1905.
186 Just then, the phone . . . MK, 67.
187 While Harriman was on . . . RH, photo opposite page 64.
188 The desk itself . . . RH, photo opposite page 25.
189 "It sounds like a good . . ." RH, 13.
190 "My secretary takes care . . ." JCMcK3, Aug. 15, 1905.
191 "We can talk in . . ." JCMcK1, Aug. 12, 1905.
192 Behind his glasses . . . MK, 215.

193 Just as McKnight . . . MK, 67.

5. Hawaii: Sugar and Surf

194 All they could see . . . ARL, 78.
195 "I quite like Alice . . ." SAC, 128.
196 He was not so sure . . . SAC, 130.
197 When SS *Manchuria* . . . Lafayette Young, "Taft Hears All About Coolie Labor in Hawaii," *Des Moines Capital,* Aug. 25, 1905.
198 Propriety dictated . . . ARL, 77.
199 Members of the party . . . ARL, 77-78.

6. Tokyo: Fateful Conversation

200 Nick looked at Alice . . . ARL, 130.
201 Alice found her . . . ARL 75.
202 Ten days after . . . Lafayette Young, "Reception of Taft Party at Tokyo," *Des Moines Capital*, Aug. 30, 1905.
203 Yokohama greeted them . . . ARL, 79-80; LG, 258.
204 The war had been grueling . . . EPT, 88.
205 Lloyd Griscom, the U.S. minister . . . LG, 238.
206 At the Tokyo station . . . ARL, 80.
207 The Japanese invited Alice. . . LG, 257.
208 Alice gratefully declined . . . ARL, 80.
209 Herbert Parsons noted . . . RZL, 70-71.
210 The emperor provided . . . ARL, 83.
211 He explained that . . . LG, 258-259.
212 The Griscoms took their . . . LG, 237.
213 On the designated day . . . MT, 94.
214 As a guest of honor . . . ARL, 84.
215 Not quite so magical . . . ARL, 84.
216 The Americans had been . . . LG, 59.
217 Social events aside . . . DB 46-47, 126-127;
218 Social events aside . . . DB, 46-47, 126-127; for a copy of the original memorandum, see "The Taft-Katsura Agreed Memorandum," July 29, 1905, accessed January 28, 2021, https://www.icasinc.org/history/katsura.html.
219 In the meantime . . . JP, 238.
220 They'd only been . . . LG, 260.
221 Alice appreciated that . . . ARL, 86.

Part V: In Boats Large and Small, August 1905

1. Oyster Bay: Historic Introductions

222 For Theodore Roosevelt . . . EM, 410
223 His goal had been . . . EM, 393.
224 The past weeks had . . . RAE, 47-50.
225 Jutaro Komura, the Japanese . . . RAE, 4.
226 Because he had openly spoken . . . EPT, 76

227 From 1877 to 1897 . . . "Sergei Witte," Spartacus Educational, accessed January 15, 2021, https://spartacus-educational.com/RUSwitte.html.

228 Witte had counseled against . . . "Russian Invasion of Manchuria," authored by *World Heritage Encyclopedia*, published by Gutenberg Self-Publishing Press, accessed January 26, 2021, http://self.gutenberg.org/articles/eng/Russian_invasion_of_Manchuria.

229 The delegates had arrived . . . EPT, 121.

230 Komura was short . . . EM, 403.

231 Witte, on the other hand . . . EM, 114-117.

232 Both delegates were termed . . . EPT, 70.

233 At the buffet luncheon . . . EM, 407-408.

2. Manila: Public Appearances

234 A Japanese newspaper . . . SAC, 120.

235 . . . and Taft wrote . . . SAC, 122.

236 Perhaps the *banzai*s . . . SAC, 122.

237 The architecture's Spanish flavor . . . MB1, 434-436.

238 Pictures of presidents . . . MB1, 435.

239 The family quarters on . . . ARL, 86.

240 The Ide girls . . . "Birthday present from Robert Louis Stevenson still treasured in Galway," *The Irish Times*, https://www.irishtimes.com/culture/birthday-present-from-robert-louis-stevenson-still-treasured-in-galway-1.1119021, December 2, 2000, accessed January 27, 2021.

241 Alice found the Ide girls . . . MT, 118.

242 The Filipinos well remembered . . . DB, 29.

243 Later he became . . . Rod Paschall, "Folly in the Philippines," HISTORYNET, accessed January 27, 2021, https://www.historynet.com/arthur-macarthur.

244 By the late 1890s . . . "The Philippine-American War: 1899-1902," accessed January 18, 2021, https://history.state.gov/milestones/1899-1913/war.

245 MacArthur still conducted . . . Rod Pascall, "Folly in the Philippines," HISTORYNET, accessed January 27, 2021, https://www.historynet.com/arthur-macarthur.

246 Because the Catholic Church . . . DB, 35-37.

247 Forty years would . . . DB, 34.

248 Once in Manila . . . SAC, 122.

249 At one reception . . . ARL, 87.

250 On the Monday . . . MB1, 437.

251 On August 30 . . . "History of the Philippine Red Cross," Philippine Red Cross La Union, accessed January 18, 2021, https://www.redcrosslaunion.org.ph/who-we-are/.

252 Alice's maid, Anna . . . MT, 89.

253 Mabel, like Alice . . . MB1, 438.

3. Islands: Luzon to Jolo

254 When he learned . . . SC, 118.

255 Built as a . . . Patrick McSherry, "The Army Transport Service," The Span-

ish-American War Centennial Website, accessed January 22, 2021, https://spanamwar.com/transports.htm.

256 The sugar-growing . . . MB1, 448-440.

257 Taft was sympathetic . . . Lafayette Young, "Return of Taft Party to Manila," *Des Moines Capital*, Oct. 28, 1905.

258 The banquets feature . . . MB1, 441.

259 Alice was always . . . ARL, 88.

260 Lafayette Young was . . . Lafayette Young, "Bridge Named for Miss Alice," *Des Moines Capital*, Oct. 25, 1905.

261 By speech time . . . ARL,88.

262 As in many places . . . Boardman1, 441.

263 Ashore, the travelers . . . Boardman1, 443.

264 Jolo's police force . . . ARL, 89.

265 Alice, Taft, their . . . ARL, 89-90.

266 Lafayette Young observed . . . Lafayette Young, "Return of Taft Party to Manila," *Des Moines Capital*, Oct. 28, 1905.

267 He sultan entertained . . . ARL, 90.

268 Later, back aboard . . . Lafayette Young, see note 275.

269 Alice was quite . . . SAC 122.

270 One of the swimmers . . . "Sultan of Sulu Offers to Wed Miss Roosevelt," *The New York Times,* Aug. 22, 1905.

4. San Francisco: Mixed Emotions

271 Cal McKnight stood on the deck . . . JCMcK3, Aug. 19, 1905.

272 A day or so earlier . . . JCMcK3, Aug.15 (evening) 1905.

273 While McKnight was . . . JCMcK3, Aug. 19, 1905.

274 He had earned . . . MK, 65.

275 His enemies viewed . . . MK, 334-335.

276 Harriman's father was . . . MK, 32-35.

277 In 1879 he . . . MK, 45.

278 Through shrewd and persistent . . . MK, 163, 446.

279 Harriman told McKnight . . . JCMcK3, Aug. 19, 1905.

280 As the ship . . . JCMcK4 Aug. 19, 1905.

281 As the children . . . MK, 298.

282 Young Mary Harriman's . . . ARL, 106-107.

5. Oyster Bay: Sticking Points

283 His fellow Harvard . . . EM, 410.

284 The principal negotiators . . . EPT, 125-126.

285 The Japanese . . . RAE, 24.

286 On August 10 . . . RAE, 83.

287 Count Witte kept . . . RAE, 89.

288 The two sides . . . EPT, 127.

289 After several intense . . . EPT, 136-137.

290 They disposed of other . . . EPT, 138.

291 Some also believed . . . RAE, 11,138.

292 Five hundred mountainous . . . EPT, 137.
293 Both Komura and . . . EPT, 110.
294 Nicholas believed he . . . EPT, 5-6.

6. Islands: Mindanao to Luzon

295 Frances Pershing's husband . . . JP, 146-205.
296 Some of the party . . . ARL, 89.
297 The trail led . . . MB1, 443.
298 For this trek . . . JP, 238-239.
299 To reach Camp Keithley . . . MB, 444.
300 Cebu was first . . . MB1, 445.
301 Lafayette Young noted . . . Lafayette Young, "Return of Taft Party to Manila," *Des Moines Capital*, Oct. 28, 1905.
302 Aboard *Logan* again . . . MB1, 445.
303 Nevertheless, with her . . . RLZ, 72-73.
304 Now, in the grand . . . Lafayette Young. See note 271.
305 On a cloudless morning . . . MB1, 445.
306 After a difficult landing . . . Lafayette Young, "Bridge Named after Miss Alice," *Des Moines Capital*, Oct. 25, 1905.
307 For their final . . . ARL, 90-91.

7. Midway and Hawaii: Island Pleasures

308 With both the line's . . . JCMcK2.
309 While the ship . . . JCMcK3, Aug. 25, 1905.
310 He found the . . . JCMcK3, Aug. 25, 1905.
311 That evening, while . . . JCMcK3, Aug. 25, 1905.
312 *Siberia*'s captain approached . . . JCMcK2; JCMcK3, Aug. 25, 1905.
313 The boats eased . . . JCMcK3, Aug. 25, 1905.

8. Portsmouth: Reluctant Compromise

314 "Peace!" The word . . . RAE, 160-161.
315 After three weeks . . . RAE, 156.
316 Baron Jutaro Komura . . . RAE, 156.
317 Although after he'd introduced . . . EPT, 122.
318 The mantra of these . . . EPT, 37.
319 Witte was not shy . . . EPT, 113.
320 By mid-August . . . EM 413.
321 The tsar ordered . . . RAE, 158.
322 Meanwhile, Roosevelt was . . . EPT, 145; EM, 410-413.
323 He spent hours . . . RAE, 142-143.
324 Roosevelt refused to . . . EM, 413.
325 Within hours, Meyer . . . EPT, 144-146.
326 Roosevelt fired a fusillade . . . EPT, 148.
327 The negotiating session . . . EPT, 155.

Part VI: Riots and Royalty, September 1905

1. Yokohama: Colorful Evening

328 The shoguns' legacy . . . AW, 70.

329 In the 1860s . . . AW, 236.

330 The treaty with . . . AW, 85.

331 Though ostensibly democratic . . . *Encyclopedia Britannica*, Fifteenth edition, Vol. 22, 1998, 297-299.

332 The governing alliance . . . James Huffman, "The Meiji Restoration Era, 1868-1869," Japan Society, accessed January 19, 2021, https://aboutjapan.japansociety.org/content.cfm/the_meiji_restoration_era_1868-1889.

333 As soon as . . . JCMcK3, Sept. 3, 1905.

334 As yet, strict censorship . . . JCMcK4 Untitled account of the Tokyo riots, 2.

335 A Pacific Mail launch . . . JCMcK2, 23.

336 But it was time . . . JCMcK1, 3-4.

2. Tokyo: Discontented Rumblings

337 On September 3 . . . JCMcK2, 37.

338 Segments of the press . . . Baronne Eleanora Mary D'Anthethan, *Fourteen Years of Diplomatic Life in Japan* (London: Stanley Paul & Co., 1912).

339 Meanwhile, the Griscoms . . . JCMcK1, 3.

340 In the meantime . . . JCMcK1, 6.

341 Emotions ran high…JCMcK3, Sept. 4, 1905.

342 Harriman responded to…JCMcK1, 10-A-10-B.

3. Canton and Hong Kong: Distant Views

343 The Taft party . . . ARL, 91.

344 Although the Boxer . . . JB, 291-292.

345 Then in 1902 . . . JB, 287-288.

346 Chinese people already . . . JB, 278.

347 Anger that was simmering . . . JB, 276. Also "Sultan of Sulu Offers to Wed Miss Roosevelt," *The New York Times*, Aug. 22, 1905.

348 Taft felt they were . . . Lafayette Young, "Lafayette Young Visits City of Hong Kong," *Des Moines Capital*, Oct. 28, 1905.

349 The Cantonese boycott . . . JB, 276.

350 In his speech . . . DB, 51.

351 In the month . . . ARL, 91-92.

352 Despite these tensions . . . SAC, 123.

353 The party left . . . ARL, 92.

354 Their time in Hong Kong . . . ARL, 91.

355 He'd confided in . . . SAC, 128-129.

356 Secretary Taft and . . . ARL, 92.

4. Tokyo: Frustrated Protesters

357 Cal McKnight was in a jinrickshaw . . . JCMcK3, Sept. 6, 1905.

358 Hibiya Park had . . . "Hibiya Park," Japan Visitor, accessed January 12, 2021,

https://www.japanvisitor.com/japan-parks-gardens/hibiya-park.
359 The mob continued . . . JCMcK2, 39.
360 "Later in the afternoon . . ." JCMcK2, 41-42.
361 The dinner was . . . JCMcK3, Sept. 6, 1905.
362 A suspenseful hour passed . . . LG, 262.
363 Two companies of soldiers . . . JCMcK2, 48-49; JCM3, Sept. 6, 1905.

5. Taku Bar: Surreal Afternoon
364 Alice and her friends . . . and *Decatur.* "Reminders of the Boxer Rebellion," *Des Moines Capital,* Sept. 15, 1905.
365 At midnight, the U.S. consul . . . warm welcome. "Reminders of the Boxer Rebellion," *Des Moines Capital,* Nov. 4, 1905.

6. Peking: Imperial Welcome
366 Alice was in . . . ARL, 94.
367 To travel the sixteen . . . MB2, 824.
368 When they had . . . ARL, 94, 100.
369 Alice had settled . . . ARL, 94-95.
370 Hoping she hadn't . . . MT, 87-88.
371 Ten women and . . . MB2, 824.
372 The audience-seekers . . . MB2, 824; JC, 16.
373 She somehow managed . . . JC, 2.
374 As regent, Cixi . . . JC, 48-49.
375 On the other hand . . . JC, 371.
376 Cixi had several . . . JC, 312-324.
377 With Mrs. Rockhill to . . . MB2, 824.
378 As she drew closer . . . ARL, 96.
379 Gold-sheathed fingernails . . . MB2, 825.
380 After Mrs. Rockhill presented . . . MB2, 825.
381 Alice had time . . . ARL, 99.
382 Mr. Wu had been interpreting . . . ARL, 99-102.
383 What the Americans did not realize . . . JC, 337.
384 After the empress withdrew . . . ARL, 100-101.
385 While Alice had been exploring . . . "William Howard Taft to American Minister Peking, 9-14-1905," William Howard Taft Papers, Manuscript Division, Library of Congress.

7. Tokyo: Flaming Spider
386 The situation was worrisome . . . JCMcK3, Sept.6, 1905.
387 However, the Boxers had . . . JC, 268.
388 The nights of September 5 . . . JCMcK1, 6.
389 On the morning of September 7 . . . RAE, 185.
390 All government buildings . . . JCMcK1.
391 Harriman wanted to . . . GK2, 16-17.
392 Harriman and his family . . . JCMcK2, 54.

8. Nikko and Kyoto: Tourists and Shoppers

393 Cal McKnight was torn . . . JCMcK3, Sept. 10, 1905.

394 Courtesy of the Nippon . . . JCMcK1, 16.

395 In the mid-nineteenth century . . . "History of Kanaya Hotel," Kanaya Hotel History House, accessed January 4, 2021, https://nikko-kanaya-history.jp/en/history.

396 But although Nikko's shops . . . JCMcK3, Sept.10, 1905.

397 By three o'clock on . . . JCMcK3, Sept. 12, 1905.

398 First on the agenda . . . JCMcK1, 16.

399 Actual power to rule . . . James Huffman, "The Meiji Restoration Era, 1868-1869," Japan Society, Columbia University, accessed January 19, 2021, https://aboutjapan.japansociety.org/content.cfm/the_meiji_restoration_era_1868-1889.

400 Another member of the . . . JCMcK1, 16.

401 Just as McKnight and Dr. Lyle . . . JCMcK3, Sept. 12, 1905.

402 One evening before they . . . LG, 263-264.

403 On September 13 . . . JCMcK, 16.

404 Several high officials . . . JCMcK3 Sept. 14, 1905.

405 They traveled all night . . . JCMcK3 Sept. 14, 1905.

406 It was under the . . . JCMcK1, 17.

407 "I am told this . . ." JCMcK3, Sept. 14, 1905; descriptions are of the pictures McKnight purchased, now in possession of the author and her sister, Constance McKnight Malmar Harris.

408 A first-hand look at . . . LG, 264.

409 But Harriman was in . . . JCMcK1, 17.

9. Seoul: Sad Scenes

410 Alice's pen moved furiously . . . SAC, 131.

411 The Korean government had . . . HC, 161-163.

412 Minister Morgan and Willard Straight . . . ARL, 103.

413 On another day . . . ARL, 103-104

414 Willard Straight accompanied . . . HC, 125.

415 Both Japanese and Koreans . . . ARL, 104.

416 He penned some verses . . . MT, 91.

417 Straight was finding it painful . . . HC, 168-170, 183.

418 Straight had been assigned . . . ARL, 104.

419 When it was time to . . . ARL, 105.

420 The train eventually deposited . . . ARL, 105-106.

10. Tsu Shima Strait: Battle's Ghosts

421 When they arrived in . . . "Riots Spread to Kobe: Ito Statue Torn Down," *The New York Times*, Sept. 9, 1905.

422 To Cal McKnight . . . JCMcK3, Sept. 23, 1905.

423 On his first tour of . . . MK, 135-136.

424 The Russians had lost . . . GJ, 68-76.

425 Gentle winds and . . . JCMcK3, Sept. 23, 1905.

11. Port Arthur: War's Remains
426 *Ohio III* waited outside . . . JCMcK3, Sept. 23, 1905.
427 Early in the war . . . GJ, 27.
428 Though the war was officially . . . JCMcK, Sept. 23, 1905.
429 And, though it was nominally . . . ET, 6-7.
430 The Harrimans and their party . . . JCMcK3, Sept. 23, 1905.
431 At 203-Meter Hill . . . JCMcK3, Sept. 23, 1905.
432 The tour of the battlefield . . . RH, 15.
433 Following the tour . . . JCMcK3, Sept. 23, 1905.
434 Back in Tokyo . . . LG, 264.

12. Peking: Brief Interlude
435 Even as he walked . . . JCMcK3, Sept. 25, 1905.
436 McKnight hired a cart . . . JCMcK3, Sept. 25, 1905.
437 While the Harriman family . . . RH, 15.
438 Harriman wanted his family . . . MK, 289.

Part VII: Winding Down, October 1905

1. Seoul: Unexpected Attraction
439 Three days in Peking . . . MK, 289. Also, Rudyard Kipling, "Buddha at Kamakura," Poetry Lovers Page: British/American Poets, 1892, accessed January 21, 2021, https://www.poetryloverspage.com/poets/kipling/buddha_at_kamakura.html.
440 The visitors were hard . . . HC, 160-162.
441 They saw the emperor . . . MK, 289.
442 For Willard Straight . . . MK, 300.
443 As he shepherded the Harriman . . . MK, 300.
444 According to her younger brother . . . RH, 6.
445 Willard Straight was not . . . MK, 300.
446 Mary could see that . . . MK, 299-301.
447 Because the Japanese . . . HC, 187-188.
448 When it was time for . . . HC, 161.
449 He was there to . . . JCMcK1, 21.

2. Tokyo: No *Banzai*s Here
450 But now, although the riots . . . SAC, 126.
451 If the subject of their . . . ARL, 106.
452 Books had played . . . SAC, 31.
453 One story she'd read . . . "Forty-Seven Ronin," www.samurai-archives.com/ronin.html.
454 In early October . . . JCMcK1, 21.
455 The Harrimans' arrival . . . ARL, 106.
456 When he departed . . . MK, 89-290.
457 To his surprise, Griscom . . . LG, 264.

458 A memorandum of agreement . . . GK2, 23-26.
459 The president of the Bank . . . JCMcK1, 21.
460 They dined on lobster . . . JCMcK4, Menu from luncheon given to the Harriman party by Matsuo, president of the Bank of Japan at the Imperial Hotel, Oct. 11, 1905, in author's possession.
461 Matsuo, the host . . . JCMcK1, 21-22.
462 On another day, their . . . JCMcK1, 22-23.
463 International finance . . . JCMcK4, From McKnight's inventory of packages and luggage to go aboard Siberia for the voyage back to San Francisco, in author's possession.
464 E. H. Harriman himself was . . . RH, 15-16.
465 And in a startling turn . . . Mary McKnight Malmar, Cal McKnight's daughter, in conversation with the author.
466 Going back with Alice . . . SAC, 136-137.

3. Tokyo: Gala Farewell
467 Looking around the crowded . . . JCMcK1, 24.
468 And not just entertaining . . . LG, 258.
469 Harriman had wanted . . . LG, 264.
470 She would say, in later . . . MT, 84.
471 Cal McKnight's future . . . JCMcK3, Sept. 3, 1905.
472 Lloyd Griscom knew . . . LG, 265.

4. Yokohama to New York: Homeward Race
473 Break the speed record . . . ARL, 107.
474 The shores of Tokyo . . . JCMcK1, 24.
475 Given the adverse . . . ARL, 107.
476 The wager was a great . . . ARL, 107.
477 When the ship steamed . . . MK, 290.
478 With the Pacific record . . . MK, 290.
479 As they raced through . . . GK2, 28.
480 Only when Harriman arrived . . . MK, 29-31.
481 The railroad had contracts . . . Mary McKnight Malmar, Cal McKnight's daughter, in conversation with the author.
482 The train sped on . . . MK, 257-263.
483 Newspaper headlines screamed . . . clipping from an unidentified Chicago newspaper, Oct. 25, 1905.
484 Harriman's train had . . . "Coast to Chicago, Fifty-Five Hours," *The New York Times*, Oct. 25, 1905.
485 Because Nicholas Longworth was . . . "*Siberia* Breaks Pacific Record," *Salt Lake Tribune*, Oct. 24, 1905.
486 The train averaged . . . "Miss Roosevelt in New York," *The New York Sun,* Oct. 27, 1905.
487 She'd already sent . . . JCMcK4, draft of telegram from Alice to her stepmother, Edith Kermit Roosevelt, in author's possession.
488 A police escort accompanied . . . "Miss Roosevelt in New York," *The New York Sun,* Oct. 27, 1905.

Epilogue

489 Contrary to predictions . . . RAE, 193.
490 Hirobumi Ito went to . . . RAE, 196-197.
491 Even though Count Sergei . . . RAE, 191-192.
492 Soon after young Mary Harriman . . . HC, 183-184.
493 Straight returned to the States . . . MK, 300-302.
494 Following the Japanese . . . HC, 199.
495 Harriman kept in touch with . . . MK, 415, 433.
496 The rift between Harriman . . . EM, 92, 316.
497 He also struck the names . . . EM, 501.
498 When Mabel Boardman returned . . . Nicholas Lemesh, "From the Archives: Volunteer Extraordinaire, Mabel Boardman," Red Cross Chat, published April 11, 2016, accessed January 21, 2021, https://redcrosschat.org/2016/04/11/from-the-archives-mabel-boardman/.
499 In 1909, Mabel received . . . LG, 315.
500 As longtime head of Red Cross . . . Nicholas Lemesh, "From the Archives: Volunteer Extraordinaire, Mabel Boardman," Red Cross Chat, published April 11, 2016, accessed January 21, 2021, https://redcrosschat.org/2016/04/11/from-the-archives-mabel-boardman/.
501 Elsie Clews Parsons had . . . RLZ, 1-3.
502 Lloyd Griscom continued in . . . LG, 266-268.
503 Shortly after the U.S. . . . LG, 92, 446, 460-462.
504 Four years after the Far Eastern trip . . . LG, 323-324.
505 Harriman left his fortune . . . MK, 6-8.
506 Averell, the Harrimans' older . . . "Ex-Gov. Averell Harriman, Adviser to 4 Presidents, Dies," *The New York Times*, August 7, 1986, accessed January 22, 2021, https://www.nytimes.com/1986/07/27/obituaries/ex-gov-averell-harriman-adviser-to-4-presidents-dies.html.
507 Roland Harriman joined . . . ERH, 55, 63-67,102, 206.
508 Under his leadership . . . "E. Roland Harriman, N.Y. Banker, Dies," *Washington Post*, February 17, 1978, accessed January 22, 2021, https://www.washingtonpost.com/archive/local/1978/02/17/e-roland-harriman-ny-banker-dies/4410d7bf-28f1-4b47-ba13-36aadaa5450b/.
509 Young Mary Harriman . . . "Mary Harriman Rumsey," National Women's Hall of Fame, accessed January 4, 2021, https://www.womenofthehall.org/inductee/mary-harriman-rumsey/.
510 She was killed . . . MK, 298.
511 Cal McKnight did not continue . . . Mary McKnight Malmar, Cal McKnight's daughter, in conversation with the author.
512 William Howard Taft favored . . . Patricia Bauer, "Payne-Aldrich Tariff Act," Britannica, accessed January 4, 2021, https://www.britannica.com/topic/Payne-Aldrich-Tariff-Act.
513 In 1920, Taft achieved . . . "William Howard Taft Biography," Biography, last modified August 14, 2019, accessed January 22, 2021, https://www.biography.com/us-president/william-howard-taft.
514 Alice Roosevelt and Nicholas Longworth . . . ARL, 112-114; SAC, 156-161.

515 Meanwhile, Edwin Morgan. . . HC, 197-199.
516 Secretary Taft proved right . . . SAC, 273-291; 300-320.
517 Manchu, the Pekingese . . . MT, 99.
518 Alice and her father grew . . . CF, 116.
519 Alice Roosevelt Longworth . . . Howard Techmann, *Life and Times of Alice Roosevelt Longworth* (New Jersey, Prentice Hall, 1979), 240.
520 Wedding bells rang for . . . "Cockran's Wedding Plans; Will Marry Miss Ide at the St. Regis Nov. 17," *The New York Times*, Nov. 6, 1906, accessed January 22, 2021, https://www.nytimes.com/1906/11/06/archives/cockrans-wedding-plans-will-marry-miss-ide-at-the-st-regis-nov-17.html.
521 Mignon Critten, Alice's . . . S. Averitt, "A Storybook Romance," Jest Among Us Two, published June 12, 2016, accessed January 4, 2021, https://jestamongus.wordpress.com/2016/06/12/a-storybook-romance/.
524 All told, three members . . . Secretary Taft as "Cupid," *The New York Times*, December 24, 1905, accessed January 22, 2021 https://www.nytimes.com/1905/12/24/archives/secretary-taft-as-cupid-two-more-members-of-his-philippine.html.

ABOUT THE AUTHOR

Pat was born in Brooklyn and married a Virginian, and claimed she was still adjusting to the ways of living in the South. When she was fifty-three, she finally graduated from college, but before that, she had acquired a Coast Guard license to captain boats of fifty tons or less, and with a friend, produced a syndicated newspaper column on flower arranging. She spent ten years as a freelance writer for Richmond and Virginia publications. After retirement to the shores of the Chesapeake Bay, she served as a hospice volunteer, working with patients and their families in three counties. She was the mother of three, grandmother of four, and great-grandmother of four. She and her tail-less cat (Bob) lived within sight of the Piankatank River in Virginia's tidewater region.

www.ingramcontent.com/pod-product-compliance
Lightning Source LLC
LaVergne TN
LVHW010053110826
845155LV00028B/326

* 9 7 8 1 9 4 7 8 6 0 6 2 9 *